The Game of Bridge

Terence Reese

Better Bridge Now

CHES

First published in Great Britain in 2002
by Chess & Bridge Limited
369 Euston Road, London NW1 3AR

Distribution:

USA and Canada: Master Point Press
331 Douglas Avenue, Toronto, Ontario, Canada M5M 1H2;
tel: (416) 781 0351; web: www.masterpointpress.com

For all other enquiries, please contact the publishers,
Chess & Bridge Limited, 369 Euston Road, London NW1 3AR;
tel: 020 7388 2404; fax: 020-7388 2407;
email: chesscentre@easynet.co.uk; web: bridgemagazine.co.uk

British Library Cataloguing in Publication Data.
A CIP record of this book is available on request from the British Library.

ISBN 0-9530218-6-6

Typeset by
Wakewing Ltd, 73 Totteridge Lane, High Wycombe, Bucks HP13 7QA

Printed in Great Britain by
The Cromwell Press, Trowbridge

Contents

Foreword

A book for beginners written by Terence Reese really requires no explanation but there are so many on the subject that this one, even by the master, needs a certain introduction.

The purpose of this book is to provide a complete and objective account of how to become acquainted with the fascinating game of bridge. Reese is not concerned simply to give rules of thumb, as were so many authors both before and after him. He is concerned with providing a basic handbook of bridge that tells players the reasons for certain lines of bidding and play. The principles of strategy, starting with the fundamentals and working up to some quite advanced points are explained and no rules are laid down without the reasons for them being explained. Here you will find not only what to do but why you should do it.

The Game of Bridge is the basic book of any bridge player's library. It is the one I learnt from.

Mark Horton
Editor
Better Bridge Now

PART I
LEARNING TO PLAY

1
Winning Tricks at No-trumps

Most books on bridge start with the bidding, but really 'Three No-Trumps' and 'Four Spades' cannot have much meaning until one knows how tricks are won and lost and what sort of cards are needed to land such a contract.

To make Three No-Trumps, as I expect you know, you have to win nine tricks. When there are no trumps, all the suits have equal rank in the play. We will begin by looking at various combinations in a single suit that may be held by declarer and dummy.

North (Dummy)
K 7 4

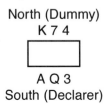

A Q 3
South (Declarer)

A simple combination that will win three tricks, no more, no less. If declarer has the lead he can play the ace, king and queen in turn and in any order.

Now add an extra low card:

North (Dummy)
K 7 4 2

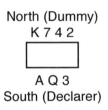

A Q 3
South (Declarer)

There are three top tricks, as before, but now the fourth card in the dummy represents a possible low-card trick, as it is called. Whether South will, in fact, make a fourth trick will depend on the distribution of the remainder of the suit. He will hope for a 3-3 break, as occurs in the following diagram:

North (Dummy)
K 7 4 2

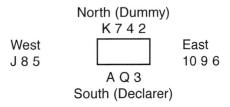

West
J 8 5

East
10 9 6

A Q 3
South (Declarer)

After the ace, king and queen have been played off, North's last card, often referred to as the 'thirteenth', will be a winner. Clearly, had the suit broken 4-2 against him, declarer would have made only his three top tricks.

Give declarer eight cards in the two hands, including the ace, king and queen, and his prospects of establishing low-card tricks will be much greater:

North (Dummy)
7 4 2

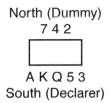

A K Q 5 3
South (Declarer)

Now South will run all five tricks without loss when the adverse distribution is 3-2. Though it is looking ahead to a rather more advanced subject, it is worth mentioning at this point that the odds are well in favour of a 3-2 break of five outstanding cards, but are against a 3-3 break of six cards.

This last diagram brings us to another common way of establishing low-card tricks. Suppose that the full distribution were:

North (Dummy)
7 4 2

West
J 9 8 6

East
10

A K Q 5 3
South (Declarer)

On the second round East would show out (that is, show void). Now South would know that he could not run five tricks, but at the same time he could be sure of establishing one long card. West must be allowed to win the third or fourth round, but South will make the remainder.

In the next example, declarer knows that he must lose at least one trick however well the cards may be breaking against him.

North (Dummy)
K 8 7 5 3

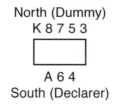

A 6 4
South (Declarer)

With five cards outstanding, including the queen, jack and ten, South cannot hope for more than four tricks. At no-trumps, if he were playing to establish this suit, he would probably give up either the first or second round, playing low from both hands. The technical name for that very common manoeuvre is 'ducking'. There are two reasons why, on most occasions, it would be better to duck an early round than to play out the ace and king: one is that by playing off the top cards you would set up two winners for the opponents if the distribution were 4-1; the other, that by playing the ace and ducking the next round you retain a high card as entry to dummy.

You may, by this time, be experiencing the slight impatience of a learner at golf who has to practise the grip and stance and wonders when he can have a hit at the ball. So, here is a full hand to play in Six No-Trumps which will give you the chance to combine some of the elements of play that we have been studying:

♠ A 7 6
♡ K 4 2
♢ A K 7 5 3
♣ K 5

♣J led

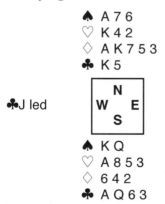

♠ K Q
♡ A 8 5 3
♢ 6 4 2
♣ A Q 6 3

The contract being Six No-Trumps, you have to make twelve tricks. West leads the jack of clubs, which does you no harm.

The first step, always, in planning the play at no-trumps is to count the certain winners. On this hand they number, in top cards, three in spades, two in hearts, two in diamonds, and three in clubs. That is ten tricks, so two more are needed. There are no other high cards that can win the extra tricks, but there are chances of finding the additional tricks in the long suit, diamonds. You have eight cards in the two hands, which means there are five against you. If they break 3-2 you can establish the suit for the loss of one trick.

That type of calculation is immediate and automatic for a player of any experience, and it is best to train yourself from the first to recognise the trick-taking potential of various simple combinations. Do not form the habit of counting up the cards of each suit as they are played. That advice is the opposite to that usually given to beginners, but the truth is that a player who has to tot up the cards after each round of a suit will never develop such talent as he may possess.

To return to our hand, South quickly assesses that he can make twelve tricks so long as he can find the diamonds breaking 3-2 against him. He must, however, take care that the opponents do not make more than one trick in the meantime. It would be very foolish to play off the aces, kings and queens in the other suits before giving up a diamond, for if that were done the enemy would have winners to cash when they gained the lead in diamonds.

The only other possible trap into which declarer could fall would be to make his winners in the wrong order. For example, suppose that he were to take the first club in hand with the queen and duck a diamond. Now the defence plays a heart and South puts on the ace. The situation is now:

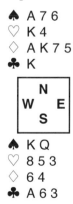

♠ A 7 6
♥ K 4
♦ A K 7 5
♣ K

♠ K Q
♥ 8 5 3
♦ 6 4
♣ A 6 3

South needs the rest of the tricks, and if the diamonds are breaking he has them safely enough. But suppose he were to make the mistake of playing off the king and queen of spades while in hand; then, in effect, he would be depriving himself of a club winner, for after crossing to dummy to make the winners there he would not be able to cash the king of clubs and then return to the ace of clubs.

There is no short rule that will enable a player to avoid this kind of entry trouble. In the position above, the singleton honour in clubs on the table, and the high spades alone in the South hand, are signs that some care is needed in the matter of going from hand to hand.

Winning tricks by promotion

We turn now to another way of establishing tricks that occurs in the play of almost every hand. This is by forcing out enemy high cards, so that cards of second and third rank held by declarer will be exalted to winning rank. As before, we will begin with the simplest example:

North (Dummy)
7 6 3

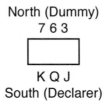

K Q J
South (Declarer)

By forcing out the ace, declarer can be sure of establishing two winners. If the opponents do not play their ace on the first round of the suit, South can play a second round.

In the next example there are two adverse winners to be forced out.

North (Dummy)
10 7 6

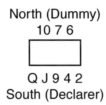

Q J 9 4 2
South (Declarer)

Now both ace and king must be conceded to the opponents but when those cards have gone South will have three winners to make.

You should be ready by now to follow the play of a complete hand on which South has to make Three No-Trumps.

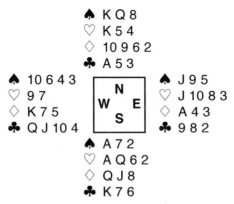

♠ K Q 8
♡ K 5 4
◇ 10 9 6 2
♣ A 5 3

♠ 10 6 4 3   ♠ J 9 5
♡ 9 7   ♡ J 10 8 3
◇ K 7 5   ◇ A 4 3
♣ Q J 10 4   ♣ 9 8 2

♠ A 7 2
♡ A Q 6 2
◇ Q J 8
♣ K 7 6

South being the declarer, West has to lead. As we shall see later when we come to study defence, it is generally sound policy for the defending side to begin with its own longest and strongest suit. On the present hand, unless clubs had been bid against him, West would normally lead the queen of clubs, choosing the top card from a sequence.

Following the prescribed practice South begins by counting his certain winners. There are three in spades, three in hearts, and two in clubs. There is a possibility of an extra trick in hearts, should that suit break 3-3. Given time, there is a certainty of two extra tricks in diamonds, once the ace and king have been forced out. We say 'given time' because at the beginning of the play South cannot be sure that he will have time to establish his diamonds before the opponents run the five tricks they need to defeat the contract.

The next stage of the general assessment that should be made at the first trick is to examine where danger lies. The weakness on this hand is evident: it is in the club suit, which the opponents have led.

Whether the opponents will be too fast and too strong in clubs to allow South to develop his diamonds at leisure cannot be determined at this point: it depends on whether the clubs are 5-2 or 4-3 and on how many entries are held by the player who has the long suit.

Having passed through the necessary and invariable stages of the planning (count the winners, look for other possible tricks, study the dangers), South is ready to consider his play to the first trick. Here we come to another pillar of play in no-trumps, the hold-up. While declarer could capture the club lead in either hand, it is better to allow the opponents to hold the first trick. The exact purpose of that manoeuvre – not actually essential to the winning of this contract – will be understood more clearly in later examples, so I will not digress now.

South lets the queen of clubs win, then, and takes the next club (for West will probably continue the suit) on the table. It would be possible, but by no means good play, to lead off three top hearts now to discover whether that suit was breaking and would provide the ninth trick. But since declarer still has a stopper in clubs, the hearts can wait; diamonds should come first.

To the third trick declarer leads a low diamond from the table. The best defence now is for East to go up with the ace of diamonds and lead his third club. By playing the ace of diamonds, East preserves his partner's entry in the suit. That is good play, because West has the long club and it would not suit the defence for West's entry in diamonds to be knocked out before the club trick had been established.

When this third round of clubs has been played, and won by the king, declarer must consider once again whether to seek his extra trick from hearts or diamonds. If it looked as though one opponent held two good clubs and the remaining entry in diamonds, he would be right to abandon the diamonds, but that possibility is in fact ruled out. Both opponents having followed to three rounds of clubs, there can be only one left. (That sort of calculation, I repeat, should be automatic. It should not be necessary to count up that twelve cards have gone – you should know instinctively that after three rounds, to which everyone has followed, there is just one card left.)

If diamonds are continued, what is the worst that can happen? The opponents have made one club (the first trick) and the ace of diamonds. If they make the king of diamonds and the thirteenth club, that will be four tricks in all and the contract will be safe.

As the cards lie, it would not affect the result if South were to cash three top hearts before leading the second diamond. That is only because the long heart is held by East and not by the player who has the diamond entry. It would, however, have been fatal for South to play the top hearts at the beginning of the hand: then East would have cashed a heart winner when in with the ace of diamonds, and that would have meant five tricks for the defence – two diamonds, two clubs and a heart.

Before leaving this had, we can perhaps look again at the hold-up in clubs, which up to now may appear to you not to have been very significant. Nevertheless, one advantage appeared when you won the third round of clubs, in that you then knew more about the distribution than you would have done if you had won the first round of clubs with the king and the second with the ace. Had you done that, you would not have been able to tell whether the suit was distributed 5-2 or 4-3, and that would lessen the confidence with which you were able to plan the rest of the play.

The hold-up would have been of real importance had the club suit been distributed as follows:

A 5 3

Q J 10 8 4   9 2

K 7 6

Now suppose that South wins the first club and plays on diamonds as before. East goes up with his ace and leads a second club, clearing the suit. South can hold up now, but it is too late: West has the second entry in diamonds, together with sufficient tricks in clubs to beat the contract.

A hold-up at the first trick makes all the difference. When East comes in with the ace of diamonds he has no clubs to lead, so declarer stays a move ahead.

This is not an altogether elementary example of hold-up play, so do not despair if it takes you a little while to master the point. The play appears in a simpler form in the next section.

Winning tricks by finesse

We have been concerned so far with the winning of tricks by force. Declarer has either had the top cards or has forced out top cards held by the opposition. Another way of coming to extra tricks is by taking advantage of the positional factor. This is the play known as a finesse, and this is the simplest form:

A Q

K 6　　　　　　　　　　7 3

5 4

South leads the five from hand, West plays the six, and the queen is played from dummy. Owing to the favourable position of the king, the queen holds: the finesse has won.

The ace-queen holding in this example is called a tenace, and so, in a looser sense, is West's king-six. The two holdings have this in common, that it is more profitable to lead towards them than away from them. Obviously, in the present example, if he first lead were made from North, only the ace would take a trick.

This principle of leading towards honours rather than away from them has very wide application. North's holding in the next diagram would not be described as a tenace, but it is equally important to lead the suit from the other hand.

K Q 7 3

A 8 5　　　　　　　　　　J 10 2

9 6 4

So long as he leads twice from his own hand South can make three tricks from this combination. He begins by leading the four; West, as a rule, will play low, and the king will win. South then returns to hand in another suit and lead the six. West will probably take his ace now, and owing to the favourable break the king and seven will be good for two more tricks.

Q J 7 3

K 10 5　　　　　　　　　　A 9 2

8 6 4

Here, again, South must lead up to dummy's honours. On the first round South leads the four, fetching the five, jack and ace. When next in, South leads again towards the Q-7-3 and eventually makes both the queen and the long card.

Declarer will often have to finesse twice against the same card. These are two parallel examples:

(i)   6 4 2   (ii)   6 4 2
    A 9 7 3   Q 8 5   10 9 7 3   K 8 5
           K J 10   A Q J

In (i) South leads twice from the dummy in order to profit from the position of the queen. In (ii) he finesses twice against the king, making all three tricks.

A finesse can also be taken against two cards. The following diagrams present what are known as double finesses:

(iii)   A Q 10   (iv)   K J 7
    K J 4   9 7 6 2   A Q 6 3   10 8 4
           8 5 3   9 5 2

In (iii) the play is to lead the three and finesse the ten if West plays low. Should the ten lose to the jack, South will try a finesse of the queen next time. As the cards lie in the diagram, the ten will hold, and a subsequent finesse of the queen will produce three tricks.

In (iv) the play is substantially the same, though here, of course, one trick must be conceded to the ace.

Still more common is the combination finesse in which the player expects to lose the first round of the battle but prepares the way for a second finesse that is more likely to succeed. This is the basic position:

                   A J 10
         K 6 4   Q 9 5 3
                   8 7 2

South begins with a finesse of the ten, which will be captured by the queen. On the next round the finesse of the jack will win. As anyone who is used to odds will understand, this combination finesse represents a 3:1 on chance of establishing a second trick, for it will fail only when both cards, the king and queen, are held by East.

Many plays of this sort begin with a deep finesse. Thus, in the example above, give North the nine instead of the ten.

                   A J 9 4
        K 10 5   Q 8 3
                   7 6 2

South leads the two and West, we will say, follows with the five. Now South could put in the jack, a play that would gain if West had K-Q-x (the x standing for any small card). A better chance, however, is to begin with the deep finesse of the nine. That will lose to the queen, but on the next round a finesse of the jack will succeed; with the suit breaking 3-3, South will win three tricks. The finesse of the nine with this combination gains when West has K-10-x or Q-10-x, and that, self-evidently, is a better chance than that he should have K-Q-x.

Another combination finesse that begins with a deep play is seen in this example:

```
              K 10 8 5
   Q 7 3                    A J 4
              9 6 2
```

On the first round South should finesse dummy's eight. That loses to the jack. When next in, South leads a low card again and West plays the seven. In a sense it is a guess whether South should try the king or the ten now, but the superior play, by far, is to finesse low a second time. This method of playing the suit by way of two deep finesses gains whenever West has queen or jack, loses only when East has both those cards.

A combination finesse also arises from this frequent holding:

```
              Q 10 4
   K J 6                    A 9 8
              7 5 3 2
```

The best chance to develop a high-card trick from dummy's holding is to play West for the jack ad at least one of the top honours. As the cards lie, the finesse of the ten loses to the ace. On the next round South leads through West's king-jack up to dummy's queen-four. Given time, South will make the queen and the 'thirteenth' as well.

You will be impatient, by now, to play another full deal on which you can try out your new-found techniques.

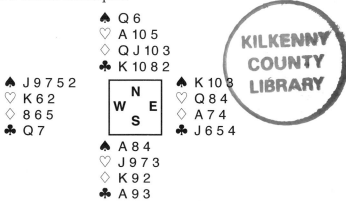

The contract is again Three No-Trumps by South. As we remarked before, it is generally sound tactics for the defence to open its longest suit. On this occasion West would lead spades, and the conventional lead from such a holding is the fourth highest card – the five.

Although, on a hand of this type, not much progress can be made in the way of counting certain winners, declarer should not neglect to make a general survey when the dummy goes down. The certain tricks in top cards number only four. There are, however, three sure winners in diamonds once the ace has been forced out. The hearts also present possibilities. This combination of A-10-x opposite J-9 has the same potential value as A-J-10 opposite x-x-x; it may well be possible to develop the suit for the loss of only one trick.

As to clubs, there too we can see the chance of an extra trick, though there will probably not be time to develop it.

Finally, if West has led away from the king of spades the queen will hold in dummy. The queen should be played for that reason, and South cannot proceed far with any plan until he has discovered the fate of that card. As the cards lie, the queen is covered by East's king.

(You may think that South would have done better to play low from dummy – that East would have had to put on the king just the same. But that is not so: East would finesse the ten, keeping his high card to kill the honour on the table.)

When East plays the king of spades on the queen at trick one South recognises that he must hold up the ace. He will have to develop tricks in the other suits and he must hope that West (who probably has the long spades) does not hold the ace of diamonds. In the hope of exhausting the short hand of spades he holds up his ace until the third round.

On this third spade a discard has to be made from dummy, and it is fairly obvious that a club is the card that can best be spared.

Now the question is whether to play on hearts or diamonds next. The diamonds will produce three certain tricks, it is true, but the hearts have to be developed as well, and South will probably have to lead them twice from his own hand; in addition, he may want eventually to be in his own hand to play off the thirteenth. Diamonds, on the other hand, can be led equally well from North or South. The right play at trick four, therefore, is to lead the three of hearts and finesse dummy's ten. Let us observe the position after that finesse has lost to the queen:

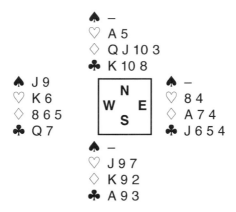

```
                    ♠ –
                    ♡ A 5
                    ◇ Q J 10 3
                    ♣ K 10 8
        ♠ J 9                       ♠ –
        ♡ K 6         ┌─────┐       ♡ 8 4
        ◇ 8 6 5       │  N  │       ◇ A 7 4
        ♣ Q 7         │W   E│       ♣ J 6 5 4
                      │  S  │
                      └─────┘
                    ♠ –
                    ♡ J 9 7
                    ◇ K 9 2
                    ♣ A 9 3
```

East, who is on lead, cannot profitably attack clubs, and his most likely play is a small diamond. He may entertain a slight hope of finding his partner with the king; in any event, the play is safe.

South puts in the nine of diamonds, which holds the trick, and pursues the hearts, leading the jack from hand. West may cover this with the king; if he does not, South will run the jack, then play another heart to the ace. The last heart will be good now, and all that South has to do is drive out the ace of diamonds. He will make, in the end, one spade, three hearts, three diamonds and two clubs.

Letting the other side lead

The club distribution on the last hand introduces a new principle – namely, that it often pays to let the opponents be the first to attack a suit. The clubs, you may recall, were originally as follows:

```
              K 10 8 2
    Q 7                     J 6 5 4
              A 9 3
```

Suppose that East, who had the lead several times, had opened up the clubs. He would have led a low card, South would play low, and West's queen would be won by the king. That would leave South with a major tenace, the ace-nine, over East's jack-six. South, in fact, would make three tricks in the suit without loss. If he has to attack the suit himself he cannot make three tricks without conceding a trick to the jack.

The same principle applies to weaker holdings. In the next diagram declarer and dummy have the cards previously held by the defenders.

```
               Q 6 4
    K 10 8                 A 9 5 3
               J 7 2
```

If declarer has to attack this suit he will make no tricks as the cards lie. If either East or West has to play first, then South will make one trick however the cards lie. Suppose, for example, that West leads the ten; dummy plays low, and if East goes up with the ace, the queen and jack will be equals against the king.

In that last example an extra trick is certain whichever opponent has to lead. With the next, very common, holding, the extra trick is certain if West has to lead, only probable if the lead comes from East.

J 6 4

A 10 5

If declarer has to attack this suit himself he will usually make two tricks only if East holds both king and queen.

If West opens up the suit, then South is assured of two tricks. He must play low from dummy, the queen or king will force the ace, and the jack and ten will then be worth a second trick.

If East leads, South will play low and West may win with the queen or king. That will leave South with a finesse position against the other honour. He will make a second trick unless both king and queen were over him from the first.

There are numerous combinations of this sort, on which the chance of an extra trick is at any rate improved by forcing the opponents to lead. Many of the tactical manoeuvres described in Part IV are designed towards that end.

Technique in finessing

Declarer sometimes has a close decision whether to take a finesse or to play for the drop of outstanding honours. This is a combination that you will have to tackle hundreds of times in your bridge career:

7 6 2

A K J 9 8 3

You can either play for the queen to drop in two rounds or you can take a finesse of the jack. This will be the winning play if East has Q-x-x.

There is an old saying, 'Eight ever, nine never', meaning that with eight cards missing the queen declarer should finesse, but with nine cards not. The first part of that saying is more true than the second. With nine cards the odds do just favour the play for the drop, but in practical play there are often indications that point to a 3-1 break.

One mistake to avoid with this combination is the finesse on the first round. The ace or king should be laid down first, for West may have a singleton queen. That is equally true when only eight cards are held, or even fewer:

A J 6 5

10 9 7 3   Q

K 8 4 2

It is apparent that if declarer leads low and finesses the jack he will make only two tricks. Playing off the king first, he brings down the singleton queen;

Another element of safety appears in the following examples:

(i)   A Q 10 6 4   (ii)   A Q 9 6 4

K 9 5 3   K 5 3 2

In example (i) the missing cards are J-x-x-x. Declarer must lay down the ace or queen first, for then he can be sure of picking up the jack, whichever opponent shows void. The second example is different, for here, if East has J-10-x-x, declarer can do nothing about it. He should therefore lay down the king first, so that if necessary he can pick up West's J-10-x-x.

In another group of safety plays, the play varies according to how many tricks are required.

A Q 7 6 4 3

9 5 2

Suppose that South needed all six tricks. He would have to finesse the queen, playing for West to hold K-x. But suppose that South could afford to lose one trick: then he would have to play differently, as will be seen from a comparison of these two diagrams:

(iii)   A Q 7 6 4 3   (iv)   A Q 7 6 4 3

K 10 8   J   J 10 8   K

9 5 2   9 5 2

If the cards lie as in (iii), then a finesse of the queen will bring in five tricks and so will the play of the ace, to be followed later by a lead up to the Q-7-6-4-3. In (iv) the finesse of the queen will be fatal. So the safety play, when five tricks are needed, is to lay down the ace on the first round.

Safety plays of this sort have numerous variations. In the average text-book they occupy more space than their practical importance deserves. There can be no question, however, about the importance of another form of safety – that of leading a low card for a finesse in situations like the following:

(v)   A Q 10 4   (vi)   A J 7 3 2
      K 6   9 7 3 2   K 8   10 9 6
             J 8 5   Q 5 4

In example (v) it will cost South a trick if he leads the jack either on the first round or the second. West will cover the jack with the king and East's nine will win the fourth round. Similarly, in (vi) it can only lose to lead the queen. West will cover and East's ten will be promoted.

When a finesse is not the best play

There are some situations in which a finesse is playable but not the best way of establishing tricks. For example:

A 7 4

Q J 6 3

South can lead the queen here, and if his object is to make two tricks without losing the lead that will be the right play. But if he wants to make three tricks the finesse is a mistake: it is better to play the ace and then up to the queen-jack. Study these two distributions:

(vii)   A 7 4   (viii)   A 7 4
      K 8 5   10 9 2   10 9 5 2   K 8
             Q J 6 3   Q J 6 3

In (vii) the cards are placed as favourably as they can be, but South cannot make more than three tricks. Suppose that he leads the queen: West will cover the honour on this round or the next, and the defence will win the third round. The same tricks would be made if declarer played the ace and then towards the queen-jack.

In (viii) declarer will again make three tricks if he plays the ace and then up to the honours; but if he leads the queen and finesses he will finish with only two tricks.

The next example would also deceive an inexperienced player:

A Q 7 3
      10 8 5 4   K 9 6
             J 2

To make three tricks, the maximum, South must begin with a low card from the table. It will not help East to put up the king, beating the air. So the jack wins and South leads back a low card to the A-Q-7. He does not finesse the queen, for he can place East with the king; he ducks, playing the seven, and on the next round East's king falls under the ace. If South begins by leading the jack here, he makes a trick fewer.

The general principle, then, is that a high card should not be led for a finesse except when the intermediate cards are so strong that declarer can afford a cover by the defence (with Q-9-x opposite A-J-10-x, for example). When there is no finesse at all, follow the general policy of leading towards honour cards. If the cards lie well you can make three tricks with as moderate a holding as the following:

A 5 3

10 8 7   K J 9

Q 6 4 2

A low card away from the ace (the ace can be played first, but it is usually well to keep that control) wins three tricks when the king is in front of the queen and the suit breaks evenly. To lead the queen from hand with this combination would be a real beginner's mistake, and at page 17 you are no longer a beginner.

2

The Play in a Suit Contract

It is time, now, to study the factor of trumps. You probably know what is meant by having one suit as trumps: it means that any card of that suit (subject, of course, to the duty of following suit when possible) ranks above any card of any other suit. When a player plays a trump on the lead of a plain suit he is said either to trump or to ruff. As the following trick is played, one player ruffs and another overruffs:

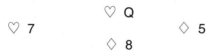

$\heartsuit$ Q

$\heartsuit$ 7 $\diamondsuit$ 5

$\diamondsuit$ 8

Diamonds are trumps and West at some point leads the seven of hearts. The queen of hearts is played from dummy. East, having no heart, ruffs with the five of diamonds. So far it is East's trick, but South, also having no hearts, overruffs with the eight of diamonds, making it his trick.

In the bidding both sides strive to obtain the contract in the denomination that suits them best. The advantage of playing with a strong trump suit is clearly seen in the following hand:

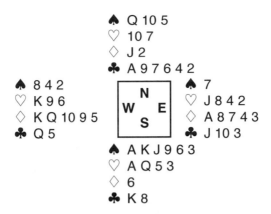

♠ Q 10 5
♥ 10 7
♦ J 2
♣ A 9 7 6 4 2

♠ 8 4 2
♥ K 9 6
♦ K Q 10 9 5
♣ Q 5

♠ 7
♥ J 8 4 2
♦ A 8 7 4 3
♣ J 10 3

♠ A K J 9 6 3
♥ A Q 5 3
♦ 6
♣ K 8

It is plain that North/South could not get far in no-trumps. Diamonds would be led and the defenders would take the first five tricks.

North/South might, however, contract for Six Spades, a small slam. From his strong holding in diamonds West would lead the king. When that won he would lead a second diamond, and now South would ruff.

In the planning of suit contracts it is often more feasible to count losers rather than winners, but on this occasion, the loser is obvious and South should consider how he is going to make twelve tricks. There are actually two possible plans and we will consider the stronger one first. There are six top tricks in spades apart from possible ruffs in dummy; then there is the ace of hearts and the ace-king of clubs. That is nine, and the obvious place to look for the extra tricks is in clubs. At no-trumps there would be a certain loser in clubs, but playing in a suit contract South can escape that loser. His plan, in brief, will be to play the king and ace of clubs, then to ruff the third round in his own hand. That will leave the remainder of the suit good if the original distribution was 3-2. Three small clubs will be established – enough for the slam.

Having noted the possibility of making twelve tricks by establishing clubs, South must study ways and means. It would be a fatal error, for example, to draw three rounds of trumps, for then after ruffing the third round of clubs South would not be able to return to the dummy.

A good sequence of play would be to draw one trump with the ace and then broach the clubs. It is true that this exposes declarer to the risk of a club ruff, but if the clubs are 4-1 he is probably going to fail anyway. As it turns out, both opponents follow to the king and ace of clubs. A third round is ruffed with the nine – a high card so that West cannot overruff. Then the two outstanding trumps are drawn by the queen and ten and the three good clubs in dummy afford discards for three hearts from declarer's hand; the heart finesse is not needed.

It was remarked at the beginning that there was another possible plan. That is to finesse the queen of hearts and ruff two hearts in the dummy. There are two reasons why that would be poor play: one is that the finesse is an inferior chance to finding a 3-2 break in clubs; the other that attempting to ruff two hearts is inconvenient in respect of entries.

To ruff in dummy is the right plan on the next hand:

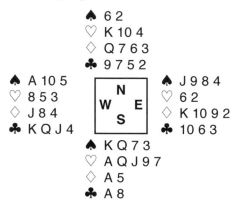

```
            ♠ 6 2
            ♡ K 10 4
            ◇ Q 7 6 3
            ♣ 9 7 5 2
♠ A 10 5          N          ♠ J 9 8 4
♡ 8 5 3                      ♡ 6 2
◇ J 8 4     W       E        ◇ K 10 9 2
♣ K Q J 4         S          ♣ 10 6 3
            ♠ K Q 7 3
            ♡ A Q J 9 7
            ◇ A 5
            ♣ A 8
```

South plays in Four Hearts and West leads the king of clubs. South can see five heart tricks in his own hand, two minor-suit aces, and a certain trick in spades. Two more are needed. The queen of diamonds is a possibility; safer is to play to ruff two spades in dummy.

While it is often right to hold up in suit play, just as at no-trumps, though mostly for different reasons, there is an objection here to holding up the ace of clubs: seeing the doubleton spade in dummy, the defence may well take the opportunity to switch to hearts in order to reduce dummy's ruffing power.

South wins with the ace of clubs, therefore. Now if it were no-trumps he would enter dummy to lead spades up to the king-queen, but dummy on this occasion has no entries outside hearts, and South is going to need the hearts for ruffs. So, the right play at trick two is the king of spades.

West will probably win and play a trump at once. (He might cash his club trick first, but since it is a trick that will not run away if South has a doubleton, it is better play to make sure of getting in this round of trumps.)

South lets this heart run up to his seven, then cashes the queen of spades and ruffs a spade. He re-enters hand with the ace of diamonds and ruffs his fourth spade. By that time he has made six tricks and has four trump winners left.

Playing a cross-ruff

The trump element is seen at its strongest on hands where the declarer takes as many ruffs as he can in both hands. That is called a cross-ruff.

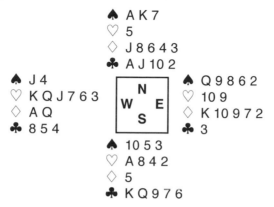

♠ A K 7
♡ 5
◇ J 8 6 4 3
♣ A J 10 2

♠ J 4
♡ K Q J 7 6 3
◇ A Q
♣ 8 5 4

♠ Q 9 8 6 2
♡ 10 9
◇ K 10 9 7 2
♣ 3

♠ 10 5 3
♡ A 8 4 2
◇ 5
♣ K Q 9 7 6

The contract is Five Clubs by South. A trump lead would work out best for the defence, but West will probably be attracted by his strong sequence in hearts and start off with the king.

It should be clear at a glance that South will not make eleven tricks if he begins by drawing three rounds of trumps. That way, he will make about nine tricks. If he could ruff three hearts on the table his only losers, on the surface, would be a spade and a diamond, and that must be the general plan.

Declarer must give thought, however, to the matter of entries. He will not want to return to hand by leading trumps, for then he will have no trumps in dummy with which to ruff the hearts. The solution is to prepare a cross-ruff by leading his singleton diamond early on.

In fact, the diamond five may as well be led at trick two. West wins, and now he may lead a trump. South lets this run up to the six, ruffs a heart in dummy, then a diamond in hand. After one more heart ruff the position is as follows:

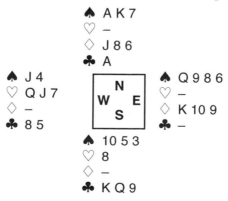

♠ A K 7
♡ —
◇ J 8 6
♣ A

♠ J 4
♡ Q J 7
◇ —
♣ 8 5

♠ Q 9 8 6
♡ —
◇ K 10 9
♣ —

♠ 10 5 3
♡ 8
◇ —
♣ K Q 9

Before continuing the cross-ruff South must cash his ace-king of spades. If he omits to do that, then West will discard a spade when the next diamond is ruffed, and South will never be able to cash the two top spades. It is a general principle of cross-ruff play that side-suit winners should be cashed early on.

Retaining trump control

So far in this chapter the declarer is a suit contract has been both long and strong in the trump suit. Often he is not, and many hands develop into a struggle between attack and defence for what is known as trump control. This is a common type of deal:

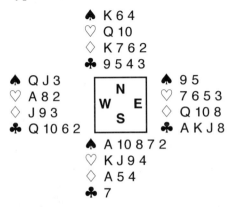

```
              ♠ K 6 4
              ♡ Q 10
              ◇ K 7 6 2
              ♣ 9 5 4 3
  ♠ Q J 3                    ♠ 9 5
  ♡ A 8 2        N           ♡ 7 6 5 3
  ◇ J 9 3    W       E       ◇ Q 10 8
  ♣ Q 10 6 2     S           ♣ A K J 8
              ♠ A 10 8 7 2
              ♡ K J 9 4
              ◇ A 5 4
              ♣ 7
```

The contract is Four Spades by South. West leads a low club; East wins and returns a club, forcing South to ruff.

First of all, let us see what happens if South plays entirely without guile. He might draw the king and ace of spades, then lead a third spade to force out the queen. West would press on with clubs and South would have to ruff with his last trump. When the defence came in with the ace of hearts West would make the fourth round of clubs and South would be one down, having lost one spade, one heart, and two clubs (not a diamond, because he throws his loser when the defence makes the last club).

Now let us play a little better from South's position. He ruffs the second club and leads out two top spades as before. He does not play a third spade, however; when the trump situation is at all shaky it is generally a mistake to continue to lead trumps when a defender has the master.

So after ace and king of spades declarer plays on hearts. West takes the ace on the first or second round, draws the queen of spades, and plays a club, forcing declarer's last trump. Now South has lost three tricks and must lose a diamond as well.

The mistake that declarer has made here is to allow West a chance to lay down the master trump, drawing two for one. The solution to this and most similar hands is to force out the important side winner – the ace of hearts – before leading off the top trumps. After ruffing the second club, then, South plays on hearts. West wins the second round and forces with another club. South ruffs, leaving this position:

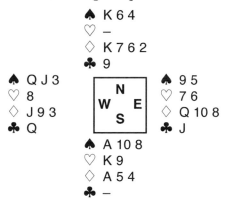

Only now does declarer play off the top spades. He continues with two good hearts, the king and nine, throwing two diamonds from dummy. Then, ignoring the master trump until it is played, he ruffs a diamond in dummy and a club in his own hand. The difference between this sequence of play and the earlier ones is that West never draws a round of trumps with his queen, but merely ruffs with it.

Another standard way of combating forcing tactics by the defence is by refusing to weaken the long trump hand. Instead, the declarer discards from side suits until dummy can take care of the suit that is being led. This is a typical example:

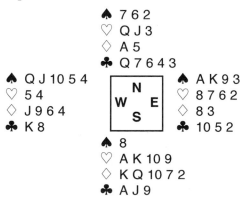

South plays in Four Hearts. West leads the queen of spades and the defence continues with a second spade. That is awkward for South because he has only four trumps and if he ruffs now he can by no means rely on drawing the outstanding trumps in three rounds. On some types of hand declarer would have to ruff and hope that the trumps would divide, but on this occasion South has a simple answer: on the second spade he throws a club, and on the third spade another club. Now dummy, the short trump hand, can take care of a spade continuation. The defenders will probably play a club. South wins with the ace, plays two top diamonds and ruffs a diamond with a high trump; then he draws the trumps and the rest of his hand is high.

Note that South did not rely on a favourable break in diamonds. Having all the high trumps he could afford to ruff the third round, guarding against a 4-2 break.

Reverse dummy play

There are some hands on which declarer will follow the opposite tactics to those of the last example: instead of declining ruffs in the long trump hand he will take as many as possible. Having shortened his own trumps in that way he will use the dummy hand to draw the opposing trumps. Such play is known as reversing the dummy.

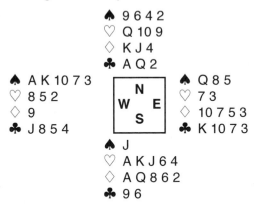

South plays in Six Hearts. The best lead for the defence is actually a club, but West is more likely to choose the king of spades. When he sees the dummy he may switch to a club, for he will not expect a second spade to stand up.

It may seem as though South must risk the club finesse, but he has in fact a stronger line of play. If he can ruff three times, and if the hearts are 3-2, he can successfully reverse the dummy.

He goes up with the ace of clubs, therefore, ruffs a spade with the six of hearts, and enters dummy with the nine of hearts. A third spade is ruffed with the king of hearts, and the jack of hearts is then overtaken by the queen. The position is now:

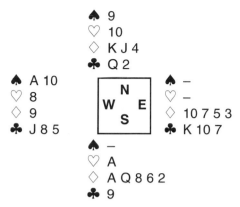

The last spade is led from dummy and ruffed with the ace of hearts. South enters dummy with the king of diamonds and draws the outstanding trump with the ten of hearts, discarding the club loser from his own hand. Then the last four tricks are won by the good diamonds.

You may wonder, where exactly did the extra trick come from? The answer is that by ruffing three times in his own hand South increased the trick-taking value of the trump suit from five (his own original holding) to six (three in dummy and three in hand).

Playing with trumps 4-4

The last two examples in this chapter are chosen not so much for what they teach about play as because they illustrate certain principles that are important in bidding. If the principle is not explained you may wonder later on why a certain form of bidding is recommended.

The first principle concerns the distribution of trumps between the two hands that normally gives the best result. You might suppose that one should always seek the trump suit that was longest: that it would be better to play with five trumps opposite three than with four opposite four. In fact, that is not so on most hands. A trump suit that is divided 4-4 will usually produce more tricks than one divided 5-3.

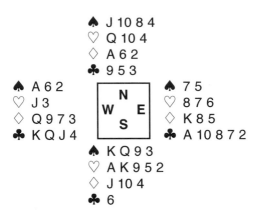

Study the play in Four Hearts against a club lead and continuation. South ruffs, draws trumps in three rounds, and forces out the ace of spades. He can make three spade tricks, the ace of diamonds, and five hearts, but will have nowhere to 'park' his two diamond losers. He will make just nine tricks.

Now consider Four Spades against the same defence. South ruffs the second club and leads the king of spades. Best defence is for West to hold off the first spade, but to take the second and play a third round of trumps. Even then, South will have no difficulty in making ten tricks. The difference is that playing in spades the club ruff gained a trick, whereas ruffing a club with hearts as trumps did not, since the long trump must make in any case. If he uses his entries to the best advantage South can in fact ruff two clubs in Four Spades and make an overtrick.

The lesson of the hand, then, is that a trump suit divided 4-4 is an admirable holding. It may even be better than 5-4, let alone 5-3. In the bidding there is often a choice whether to play in Four of a major suit or in Three No-Trumps. When the major is divided 5-3, no-trumps is often the better spot, but when the division is 4-4, there is almost always an extra trick or two to be made in the suit.

Making the weaker suit trumps

Another peculiarity in the structure of cards is that when the length of two possible trump suits is equal it will usually be better to play in the weaker suit. Once again, observe the respective fates of Four Spades and Four Hearts on the following hand:

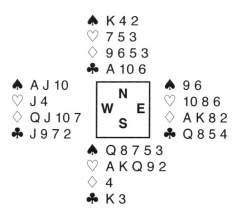

The same number of cards in each major and, as you can see, the same distribution, but the hearts are stronger in top cards. Now try Four Hearts against a diamond lead and continuation. You ruff and, better than drawing trumps at once, play on the side suit. A spade is led to the king, which holds. You lead a spade back and play low from your hand, for West appears to have the ace and it may be bare by now; at any rate, nothing can be gained by going up with the queen. Alas! The jack wins and West plays another diamond, forcing you to ruff again. You can draw trumps now, but when West comes in with the ace of spades the defence will make a diamond trick.

Four Spades, on the other hand, plays easily. You ruff the second diamond, lead a spade to the king, and duck a spade return to West's jack. The position is now:

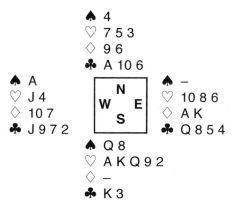

West will probably lay down the ace of spades and force again in diamonds. Since the hearts are solid, South will make the remainder.

Alternatively, West might play a diamond in the diagram position. South ruffs and plays on hearts, leaving the master trump at large. West will make his ace of spades when he wants it, but that will be all.

So the lesson of the hand is this: it is better to play with moderate trumps and a strong side suit than with strong trumps and a moderate side suit.

In the example just shown, that lesson was pointed by the loss of control in Four Hearts. Another reason why the suit that is weaker in 'tops' should generally be preferred as trumps is that declarer will then be less likely to sustain a ruff. Compare these two holdings in the major suits:

North
♠ A 10 8
♡ J 9 4

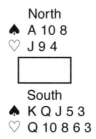

South
♠ K Q J 5 3
♡ Q 10 8 6 3

Playing in a spade contract South is exposed to a ruff in hearts. One player may have A-K-x and his partner a doubleton, or one player A-x and the other K-x-x; either way, they can come to a ruff of the third round if they lead the suit before declarer has been able to draw trumps. Playing with hearts as trumps it is much harder for the defence to negotiate a ruff in spades: they will seldom achieve it unless the spades are 4-1.

3

The Language of Defence

The declarer has the easier task in bridge. It is true that both sides can see the dummy, but it is easier to make the best of 26 cards in combination than of 13 in conjunction with a partner whose hand is concealed.

A declarer has no occasion to convey messages to his dummy, but the defenders are much concerned with exchanging information by means of signals and conventions. This exchange begins, naturally, with the opening lead.

The lead at no-trumps

There are two matters to consider: which suit to lead; and then, which card of that suit.

For the most part, the defenders to a no-trump contract should launch their strongest weapon. Time is the important factor, for most contracts depend on which side can establish its long suit first. The occasions when the leader may depart from this general principle will be discussed later. First, we will study which card the defender should lead once he has decided to lead from his longest and strongest suit. The general rule – as will appear from the table that follows – is to lead the top of a sequence (king from K-Q-J or K-Q-10) or the higher card from touching honours. When no strong combination of honours or touching cards is held, the conventional lead is the fourth highest – from K-10-7-5-2, the five.

From A-K-Q-x lead the king.

From A-K-J-x lead the king.

This is an exception to the general rule of leading the top of a sequence. Actually there is no good reason at no-trumps why the usual pattern should be changed. Many good players do lead the ace from such holdings, but the king is traditional.

From A-K-10-x-x lead fourth best.

From A-K-x-x-x lead fourth best.

The reason for leading low is seen in this diagram:

$$J\,8\,5$$
$$A\,K\,7\,4\,3 \qquad\qquad 9\,2$$
$$Q\,10\,6$$

So long as West begins with a low card, his partner will have a card to play back should he gain the lead.

From A-Q-J-x-x lead the queen.

The lead is likely to give a trick to the king, but when the leader has a five-card suit he must be willing to make this concession. The queen is led so that the suit will be established at once when declarer has something like K-10-x.

From A-J-10-x lead the jack.

This lead will take care of distributions such as the following:

(i)   9 8 3   (ii)   Q 7
    A J 10 6 4   7 2   A J 10 6 4   8 3 2
         K Q 5   K 9 5

In (i), after South has captured the jack with the king or queen, the defence will be able to run four tricks as soon as East can gain the lead. In (ii), again, the lead of the jack holds declarer to one trick.

From A-10-9-x lead the ten.

Similarly from K-10-9-x and Q-10-9-x. The advantage is seen in these diagrams:

(iii)   J 5 3   (iv)   6
    Q 10 9 4   K 6 2   K 10 9 5   Q 8 4 3 2
         A 8 7   A J 7

In (iii) declarer will stop the suit twice if West leads a low card but not if he leads the ten; for in that case, should dummy play low, so will East. In (iv) the run of the suit will be blocked if West begins with the five. After the queen has lost to the ace, East may come in to lead through the jack-seven but will require an additional entry before he can make the fifth card.

From a five-card suit headed by A-10-9 the ten is still the conventional lead, but fourth best will often turn out better.

From K-Q-J-x lead the king.

From K-Q-10-x lead the king.

From K-J-10-x lead the jack.

From Q-J-10-x lead the queen.

From Q-J-9-x lead the queen.

From J-10-9-x lead the jack.

From J-10-8-x lead the jack.

From 10-9-8-x lead the ten.

When no honour is held, fourth best is normal, but the top card may be led from a sequence such as 9-8-7-x-x and would certainly be led from 9-8-7-x. *(The fashion now is to lead the second highest card from such combinations.)*

The defender will often have a choice between suits of equal length. The consideration then will not be which suit is stronger so much as which lead is safer and more constructive. Thus, A-K-x-x, A-Q-x-x, A-Q-J-x and K-Q-x-x are all unattractive leads, likely to give away a trick unnecessarily. A strong sequence such Q-J-10-9 may well be preferred to a weak five-card suit. There is not a lot to choose between A-x-x-x, K-x-x-x, Q-x-x-x and J-x-x-x; all these holdings would be improved by the inclusion of the ten.

So much for the choice of lead once you have decided to open your best suit. Much more difficult is to judge when to abandon your long suit in favour of a shorter one. These are some general reasons why you might be inclined to do so:

1 **The opponents have bid your best suit.** In that case you will lead it only if you have a strong sequence, such as Q-J-10-9-x.

2 **Your best suit does not present a good lead and you therefore judge it wiser to make a safe lead that will give nothing away.** For example, you hold:

♠ 10 9 7
♡ A Q 6 3
◇ J 8 4 2
♣ Q 6

Neither of your four-card suits represents an attractive lead and the normal choice would be the ten of spades.

3 **Your partner has made a bid.** In that case you should lead his suit unless you have a particularly good alternative. If you have two or three small cards, lead the top one. From four cards or more, lead fourth best. From three to an honour the bottom card is usually best, as will appear from the following diagrams:

(v)   7 5   (vi)   J
    Q 9 4   K 10 6 3 2   10 8 3   K Q 7 6 4
         A J 8   A 9 5 2

In all cases the lead of the top card will cost a trick. When two honours are held, the top card is led when the honours are touching (jack from J-10-x), but usually the low card from a combination such as A-10-x or K-J-x.

4 Your hand is so weak that it seems better to try to hit partner's long suit. For example:

> ♠ 7 5 4
> ♡ J 7 2
> ◇ 8 4
> ♣ J 7 5 3 2

You have a five-card suit, but to make anything of it you will have to find your partner with a very strong holding. A better chance is to try to find his long suit. If the bidding has given no clue it is a guess which suit you should try. If you choose a heart you should lead the two, just as you would if partner had bid the suit.

The play by third hand

'Third hand' is the partner of the opening leader. The following examples show typical positions in defence:

(i)   K 8   (ii)   K 8
    Q J 9 5 2   7 3   Q J 9 5 2   10 7 3
         A 10 6 4   A 6 4

In (i) West leads the queen and the king is played from dummy. East should play the three, his lowest card, as a sign of discouragement. In (ii), whether or not the king is played from dummy, East should play the seven. Having the ten, he can read partner for the Q-J-9, so plays an encouraging card.

(iii)   9 2   (iv)   K 4
    K Q J 4   7 6 5 3   J 10 8 5 2   9 7 6 3
         A 10 8   A Q

Although East has no high card, his length entitles him to encourage in a mild way by playing a middle card on the first round and following with a lower card. To reverse in this way is called a peter or echo.

(v)   9 6 3   (vi)   8 6 2
    K Q 10 8 2   A 4   Q J 10 7 3   K 4
         J 7 5   A 9 5

When third hand has a doubleton honour, as in these two examples, he must be sure to unblock, by playing the ace on the king in (v) and the king on the queen in (vi).

(vii)		7 5		(viii)		Q 5 2	
	K J 10 3 2		A 8 4		J 10 9 3		A 8 4
		Q 9 6				K 7 6	

These two examples show the difference between 'finessing against partner', generally a mistake, and 'finessing against dummy', generally correct. When West leads the jack in (vii) it may be likely from East's point of view, that declarer has king-queen, but to withhold his ace would be disastrous as the cards lie. The position in (viii), when West leads the jack and dummy plays low, is quite different. In general, high cards should be used to kill high cards, and here East must allow the jack to run up to the king.

(ix)		8 5		(x)		7 5	
	K 10 7 3 2		Q J 4		A 10 6 4 2		Q 8 3
		A 9 6				K J 9	

In diagram (ix) third hand has touching cards, the queen and jack. Whereas the higher card is led from such a combination, the lower card is played. The reason will appear from the example. West leads the three, East plays the jack, and we will assume that South, perhaps fearing attack from another quarter, does not hold up but wins with the ace. West will then be able to place his partner with the queen, for with ace-queen South would presumably have won with the queen.

Diagram (x) shows the other side of this picture. When the queen is headed by the king West can place South with the jack, probably guarded.

The next two examples bring us to a different point – the card that third hand should return when he has won the first trick.

(xi)		7 6		(xii)		5 2	
	K 10 8 5 3		A 9 2		K J 9 4		A 10 6 3
		Q J 4				Q 8 7	

In (xi) West leads the five ad East wins with the ace. He must play back the nine, the higher of his two remaining cards. If he were to return the two instead, that would tell West that he had ace-two alone or four cards. As it is, when South puts on the queen (or jack) West can duck so as to retain communications between the defending hands. That may be very important later should East gain the lead and West have no quick entry.

In (xii) West leads the four, East wins with the ace, and should now return the three, his original fourth best. South will probably go up with the queen, his only chance being that the king also is held by East. When West takes the queen with the king he can lay down the jack, for his partner's low return has shown four cards. (East could also have ace-three alone, in theory, but that would place South with Q-10-8-7-6 – improbable if the suit has not been mentioned; also, with ace-three alone East would probably not return the suit, for the reason explained in the next paragraph.)

In considering whether he should return partner's suit or try something different, third hand must pay special attention to the exact card led. The reason for the convention of leading fourth best is to give partner a chance to estimate the distribution. As a simple example, suppose that a two is led. The leader is immediately placed with a four-card suit. In example (xi) above, East can make the same inference when the four is led, for he holds the three himself and can see the two in dummy. West cannot have a five-card suit, for if so, what can the fifth card be? With ace-three alone, therefore, East would not return the suit, for he would know that declarer had five cards against his partner's four.

By the same token, when partner leads a card such as the five and later follows with a lower card, such as the two, he can be marked with at least a five-card suit. If he produces two cards lower than the one led he shows a six-card suit.

Another help to assessing the lie of the cards after the first lead is the so-called Rule of Eleven. The leader's partner subtracts the number of the card led from eleven, and the answer tells the number of cards higher than the one led that are held by the other three players. Thus, is a six is led, there are five cards higher than the six not in the leader's hand.

The Rule of Eleven will often help a player to distinguish between a fourth best lead and top of nothing. The following are the cards of North, the dummy, and East:

	Q 9 7	
6 led		10 8 2

Subtracting six from eleven, East's first thought is that there are five cards higher than the six not in the leader's hand. However, all five are visible. The missing high cards are the A-K-J, and with such a holding West would lead an honour. The inference is that West has not led fourth best at all: he has led 'top of nothing', from some such holding as 6-5-3.

The rule is valuable in another way in this sort of situation:

	10 8	
Q J 7 5 3 2		A 6 4
	K 9	

West leads the five. East wins with the ace and returns the six. After this trick he has seen all six cards higher than the five not in the leader's hand, so knows that West has the remaining top cards.

If you wonder, 'Why eleven?' the answer is that the cards in bridge rank from two to fourteen (though the top four are represented by honours). When a player leads fourth best he has three cards higher than the one he has led; subtract three from fourteen and you arrive at eleven, that being the 'height' of the suit apart from the leader's hand.

The signals and conventions described in this section apply throughout the play and not only to the first couple of tricks. Thus at any time a peter can be used to show strength; when there is no opportunity to complete the peter, the discard of a single high card, such as a seven upwards, may be taken as encouraging. If a new suit is led by the defence in the middle of the play the same general conventions apply as to the original lead, though of course the cards visible in dummy may make a difference.

One other type of signal is that to show length rather than strength. This is used especially when the declarer is developing a long suit.

(xiii)   K J 10 7 5   (xiv)   K Q 10 9 5
      9 2   A 8 4   7 6 3   A 8 2
            Q 6 3   J 4

The general principle is that with an even number of cards, two or four, the defender should peter. In (xiii), therefore, West plays the nine on the first round. That tells East to hold up his ace until the third round – essential if dummy has no entry. In (xiv) South may lead the jack and put on the queen from dummy. Since West's three is the lowest card he can have, East will place him with three cards – neither a doubleton nor 7-6-4-3. East will know, therefore, that he should take the second round of the suit.

The lead against a suit contract

In trump contracts there is not the same urgency to establish long suits that we found at no-trumps. Only on a special type of hand – the type where declarer is liable to run short of trumps – does it help the defence to establish low-card tricks. Consequently there is not the same advantage in making opening leads from length.

Safety is an important consideration. Whereas in a no-trump contract a defender will readily lead from a holding such as A-Q-x-x-x, in a suit contract he will generally look first for a safer lead. The best lead, other things being equal, is one that is both safe and, in one way or another, constructive. Many books set out a list of recommended leads with such honourable characters as A-K-Q and K-Q-J at the top and disreputable villains like A-Q-x and K-x at the bottom. To present the matter in that way is an encouragement to lazy thinking, for many factors enter into the decision apart from the texture of the suit. First, however, we must consider the conventional leads from various holdings.

From K-Q-x-x lead the king.

From Q-J-x-x lead the queen.

At no-trumps a low card would be led from four or more cards headed by these touching honours, but against a suit contract the object is to set up immediate rather than eventual tricks.

From A-x-x-x lead the ace.

The lead from an unsupported ace is far from safe, but there are times when no other suit offers a better chance of establishing tricks. It is usual to lead the ace rather than a low card.

From K-x-x, Q-x-x, J-x-x lead the bottom card.

This type of lead, also, is liable to cost a trick. but again it may be the only suit where there seems a chance to start an attack.

From A-x, K-x, Q-x, J-x lead the honour.

These are sometimes listed as 'desperation leads'. The commonest of the four is the ace from A-x, for this will often lead to a ruff.

From 7-5-3 lead the seven.

This 'top of nothing' lead is safe and often preferable to leading from an honour combination. (*Again, the modern style is to lead the five.*)

Short-suit leads

There remain some types of lead that have no parallel at no-trumps. One is the short-suit lead, made primarily in the hope of obtaining a ruff. A lead from a doubleton is stronger than from a trebleton because a ruff may follow. A doubleton or singleton lead has a better chance of success when the defender has a trump trick, as on the following hand:

♠ K 10 7 2
♡ A 7 3
♢ Q 10 8 5 2
♣ 6

If West has to lead from this hand against Four Hearts his likely choice will be the six of clubs. Should partner have the ace he may win and return a club for an immediate ruff. Since West has a trump trick there is a chance of a ruff even if partner does not hold the ace of clubs: West can win the first or second round of trumps and may find partner with an entry in spades or diamonds.

Forcing leads

If the contract on the hand above had been Three or Four Spades the singleton lead would not have been so strong, since West would have two likely trump winners in any event. A better defence might be to play what is known as a forcing game: to lead diamonds, the long suit, and hope to weaken the declarer's trump position by forcing him to ruff more often than he can afford.

Trump leads

It is often sound play to lead the trump suit itself, either for safety or with the idea of preventing the declarer from making his trumps separately. From a holding such as 8-6-3 in the trump suit a low card should be led, for the higher one will sometimes acquire some value as the play develops.

The lead against a slam

Against a slam contract, more than any other, the lead depends not on the holding in individual suits but on the general defensive plan. Especially when it seems that the declarer in a small slam has a side suit to develop, an attacking lead from a king or a queen may be called for. The defence will try to set up a quick trick before declarer has forced out the one certain winner in the defending hands.

Conventions in the later play

The same signals for showing strength and weakness are used in suit play as at no-trumps, and the same convention is followed of leading the top card of a sequence and playing the bottom one.

Very common in suit play is the peter to show a doubleton. If often occurs on the opening lead:

(i)		J 7 3		(ii)		J 7 4	
	A K 5 4		8 2		K Q 10 6 3		8 5
		Q 10 9 6				A 9 2	

In (i) West leads the king and East played the eight. Reading this as a come-on signal, West continues with the ace and gives his partner a ruff on the third round. In the second example West's king loses to the ace, but if the defenders gain the lead before trumps are drawn they can ruff out the jack after East has signalled with the eight and five.

When partner shows that he can ruff it is generally right for a defender to continue a suit even though declarer may be able to overruff. That is clearly the best defence on the following hand, which illustrates various forms of defensive signalling:

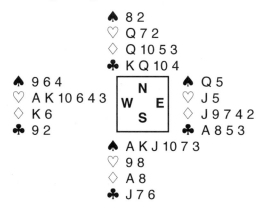

♠ 8 2
♡ Q 7 2
◇ Q 10 5 3
♣ K Q 10 4

♠ 9 6 4   ♠ Q 5
♡ A K 10 6 4 3   ♡ J 5
◇ K 6   ◇ J 9 7 4 2
♣ 9 2   ♣ A 8 5 3

♠ A K J 10 7 3
♡ 9 8
◇ A 8
♣ J 7 6

South plays an optimistic contract of Four Spades. West leads the king of hearts and East begins a peter by playing the jack.

(Digressing for a moment, it is usual to peter with J-x, but not with Q-x. The play of the queen under partner's king shows either a singleton or a combination headed by queen-jack.)

West can calculate that if East has a doubleton, so has South. However, it is advisable to continue the suit in order to kill dummy's queen. So West continues with the ace of hearts and a small one.

Although it does not affect the result of this hand, an important principle arises here. East may realise, especially if his partner has overcalled in hearts, that he is going to be overruffed. Nevertheless, he should put in his high trump, the queen. Suppose that partner had held 10-x-x or, possibly, J-x; then the queen, if overruffed, would promote a trump trick in partner's hand.

As it happens, South can overruff the queen without danger to his trump holding. He does so and plays three rounds of trumps to draw the trumps against him. A diamond is thrown from dummy on the third round. East has to discard twice. On the second round he discards the two of diamonds, suggesting that he has no high honour in this suit. On the third round he may throw the five of clubs, preparing a high-low signal to show strength, The position is now:

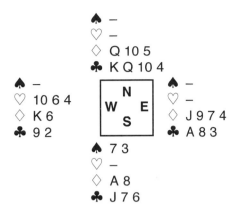

```
              ♠ —
              ♡ —
              ◇ Q 10 5
              ♣ K Q 10 4
  ♠ —         ┌─────────┐      ♠ —
  ♡ 10 6 4    │    N    │      ♡ —
  ◇ K 6       │ W     E │      ◇ J 9 7 4
  ♣ 9 2       │    S    │      ♣ A 8 3
              └─────────┘
              ♠ 7 3
              ♡ —
              ◇ A 8
              ♣ J 7 6
```

South leads the six of clubs to dummy, and West plays the nine. That tells East that he must hold up his ace until the third round. In the end the defence will win a diamond trick and South will be one down.

There are two further signals that might have been used on this hand, though they would not have affected the result. One was at trick three when West, it will be recalled, was leading a heart which he knew was going to be ruffed. His hearts at that point were the 10-6-4-3 and it could make no practical difference which one he led. In such a situation he could have made what is known as a suit-preference signal. By leading an unnecessarily high card, such as the ten, he could have shown strength in the higher ranked of the outstanding suits – diamonds and clubs. Thus, for a partnership using the convention (and all good players do use it) the ten would be the right card to play, in view of the honour card in diamonds; the three would suggest some values in clubs.

The other signal that might have been used was the 'trump echo'. In the trump suit only, a peter shows not a doubleton but three cards. Thus, West could have petered with the six and four to give partner an early count of the trumps. For the most part, however, this trump echo is reserved for occasions when a defender wants to convey to his partner that he can ruff some suit if the trumps are not drawn. It would not to do to peter every time one had three trumps, for that would be too helpful to the declarer.

That last remark perhaps echoes a thought that may have been in the reader's mind since the beginning of this chapter. These various signals to strength and weakness, shortness and length: are they not just as helpful to declarer as to the other defender?

Of course, experienced players do not send forth signals on every occasion: they know that in many situations partner will be able to work out what is wanted from knowledge of his own hand. A convention like leading fourth best certainly tells a tale and has, indeed, often been attacked on those ground; but while it may give information to declarer, that information is more often the writing on the wall than the means of presenting him with his contract. In general, it is more important to inform partner than to withhold information from declarer. That is the case for conventions; it would certainly be very difficult to play the defence without them.

PART II
LEARNING TO BID

4

Valuation and Opening Bids of One

A bridge hand can be interesting in two ways: it may be strong in honour cards or strong in playing values; and it may, of course, be strong in both. Compare these two holdings:

(i)   ♠ K 10 8 4   (ii)   ♠ 6 4
      ♡ A Q 7 3   ♡ K J 8 6 4 3
      ◇ K 7   ◇ –
      ♣ J 9 6   ♣ Q 10 9 7 2

Hand (i) is a king above average in terms of high cards; a simple calculation, for it possesses an ace, king, queen, jack and a ten, and a king in addition. Hand (ii) is an ace below average in terms of high cards but possesses strong distribution.

You could not say, at the outset, which was the 'better' hand. It all depends on the 'fit': that is to say, whether the second hand fits with partner in one or other of the long suits.

In general, opening bids of One are made on the first type of hand, the one containing the high cards. This is because the honour cards, likely to win tricks whatever the declaration, represent solid and unchanging value: they are the gold that you bring to market.

The reason why, in principle, one does not open on the purely distributional type of hand is that should partner have something to say, but not fit at all with your hand, the bidding will soon go out of control. Where the distribution is even stronger than on hand (ii) above, a different type of opening bid can be made – a bid of Three or Four; we shall come to that later.

It was observed that hand (i) was a king above average. That, however, is not the standard way of assessing a hand. There is a more convenient system, known as the 'point count'.

This is a short way of estimating high-card values and it works by assigning a numerical value to each honour card. The simplest and most popular count is as follows:

$$
\begin{array}{lcl}
\text{ace} & = & 4 \text{ points} \\
\text{king} & = & 3 \text{ points} \\
\text{queen} & = & 2 \text{ points} \\
\text{jack} & = & 1 \text{ point}
\end{array}
$$

Opening bids of one

To open the bidding, a player should have rather more than his fair share of high cards. To some extent, good distribution and playing strength will compensate for lack of honours, but it is not usual to open with a bid of One on less than an average hand.

The average point-count is self-evidently ten – representing one ace, one king, one queen and one jack.

Vulnerability, position at the table (whether dealer, second, third or fourth in hand), and intermediate cards (such as tens and nines), all have a bearing on opening bids, but in so far as one can summarise these are the minimum standards:

With a hand that is weak in playing strength, containing no suit of more than four cards: 12–13 points.

With a fair five-card suit, headed by at least two honours: 11–12 points.

With a good suit, or two fair five-card suits: 10–11 points

Hands with one long suit present the least problem, so we will look at some of those first.

(i) ♠ K Q J 10 7 4   (ii) ♠ 6 3 2
      ♡ 6   ♡ Q 8 6 5 4 2
      ◇ A 7 5 2   ◇ K J
      ♣ 9 4   ♣ A J

Hand (i) is a sound opening bid in any position and at any score. The main suit is strong and can safely be rebid even if not supported. The hand would be reckoned to contain about 6½ playing tricks, for clearly the spades are worth five tricks in a spade contract and the diamond combination is worth at least a trick and a half.

Hand (ii), though it contains a point more, is by no means as strong. The suit is weak and will require support; apart from the long suit the distribution is dead, and the hand contains many losers. This would not be a good opening first or second in hand. While many players would open third or fourth in hand, hoping for a partscore, it would by no means be wrong to pass.

(iii) ♠ 6 3
♥ A K J 10 7
♦ K 9 6 4
♣ 7 3

(iv) ♠ K J 8 6 3
♥ A 4
♦ Q 8 3
♣ K 7 2

These are minimum openings for a hand with one five-card suit. Hand (v) has only 11 points, but the suit is good and the fact that the side king is in a suit of four cards improves the playing strength. Hand (vi) has flat distribution and the suit is indifferent but the high cards justify an opening.

When a hand contains only four-card suits, the normal standard is 12-13 points. These balanced hands are opened One No-Trump. It is convenient to take no-trump openings and responses together, so examples of such hands are postponed to a later chapter.

When there is a choice of suits

On two-suited hands there are two general rules:

With two suits of equal length, open with the higher ranking

When one suit is longer than the first, bid the longer suit first.

There are many exceptions to both these rules, but we will take the easy hands first.

(i) ♠ Q 10 7 5 2
♥ A K J 6 4
♦ K 5
♣ 3

(ii) ♠ A Q J 4
♥ K 3 2
♦ K Q 7 5
♣ Q 7

On hand (i) the beginner's instinct may be to open One Heart because it is the stronger suit. There are two reasons why that is wrong. The first is that it makes the development of the bidding more difficult. Should the bidding go, for example, 1♠ – 2♣ – 2♥, the responder (that is, the opening bidder's partner) can show preference for spades without raising the level of the bidding; but if the sequence is 1♥ – 2♣ – 2♠, then responder must go to Three Hearts to show preference. The other reason why it would be misguided to open One Heart is that, as we saw in the last example of Chapter 3, there is no advantage in making the stronger suit trumps: given equal length, it is better that the weaker suit should be trumps.

On hand (ii) the natural opening bid is One Spade. In some systems an opening bid of a major shows five cards, but that is a special convention.

In general, however, a major-suit opening is undesirable on a suit weaker than A-10-x-x or Q-J-x-x.

	(iii)	♠ K Q 8 4		(iv)	♠ 6
		♡ 7 2			♡ A K 8 6 3
		◇ A K 9 6 3			◇ J
		♣ A 6			♣ K J 8 7 5 3

These hands illustrate the other general rule – that the longer suit should be bid first. Thus, on hand (iii), the opening is One Diamond, on hand (iv) One Club.

It was remarked that there were many exceptions to both principles for bidding two-suited hands. When there are five cards in clubs and spades, One Club is often preferred; and on moderate hands containing two four-card suits it is often right to open the lower-valued.

	(v)	♠ K Q 8 6 3		(vi)	♠ A Q J 6
		♡ J 4			♡ K J 9 4
		◇ 4			◇ 6 3
		♣ A K 10 7 3			♣ A 7 2

It is clear that on hand (v), a moderate two-suiter, time is saved by opening One Club. The bidding might go: 1♣ – 1♡; 1♠ – 2◇; 2♠. Now the opener has bid his spades twice without going beyond the two level since with five spades and four clubs he would have opened One Spade he has shown five cards in both black suits while keeping the bidding low.

With hand (vi), a balanced hand, opener wants to find a 4-4 fit in a major suit is there is one, otherwise to play in no-trumps. If One Spade is opened, a heart fit may be missed (as we shall later, partner needs a five-card suit to respond Two Hearts to One Spade); however, over One Heart partner will bid One Spade with four (unless he has a strong hand with a longer minor suit), so the spade fit cannot be lost.

On 4-4-4-1 hands there is a general rule in favour of bidding the suit below the singleton, but such hands – indeed, all hands – must be judged on their merits.

	(vii)	♠ A Q 8 3		(viii)	♠ A K 10 6
		♡ 5			♡ A Q J 3
		◇ K Q 4 2			◇ 7
		♣ A Q 10 7			♣ K J 5 2

On (vii) One Diamond, anticipating a One Heart response, is the most economical opening, but it would not be wrong to open One Club. On (viii), open One Club and rebid One Heart if partner responds One Diamond.

The exceptions to the other main principle – that the longer suit should be bid first – occur mostly on moderate hands when the suits are adjacent.

(ix) ♠ A 5 3   (x) ♠ 6
    ♡ A K J 6   ♡ K Q 10 7 4
    ◇ 9 6 5 4 2   ◇ A J 7 5 3 2
    ♣ 4   ♣ 4

On hand (ix), to open One Diamond would necessitate a rebid of Two Diamonds on that miserable suit if partner responded Two Clubs. It is better to open One Heart; if partner responds One Spade, you raise to Two Spades, while over Two Clubs you can rebid Two Diamonds. On (x) One Heart is preferable to One Diamond, though if the hand were stronger One Diamond would be correct.

The limits of opening one bids

Most of the hands in this chapter have been comparatively weak. The range for opening bids of One goes up to about 21 points when the distribution is not strong. The stronger openings, Two Clubs (conventional and forcing to game) and Two of the other suits, are discussed in Chapter 8.

5

The First Response to
Bids of One

Although they can be strong, opening bids of One are also limited and
responder is always free to pass on a weak hand. For the most part, he
should pass when hc has fewer than 6 points; this can be reduced when he
has a fair suit which he can bid at the level of One.

(i) ♠ 7 6 3
♥ Q 10 7 6 4 2
♦ J 8 4
♣ 7

(ii) ♠ 6 4
♥ K J 9 7 6
♦ 5 3
♣ J 8 6 2

On (i) responder could raise an opening bid in hearts, but he should
pass any other call. Some players would be reluctant to pass One Club.
'Partner might have only four clubs,' they say. It is true that in that case
it would be an improvement to bid One Heart, but that will not be the
end of the matter. Partner will perhaps jump in no-trumps or double
some call by the opponents on the strength of your bid. One might
quote in this connection a wise remark by a brilliant writer on the game,
the late S J Simon: 'You must not play for the best possible result on
every hand,' he said, 'but the best result possible.' That means, in
relation to the present hand, that very likely there is a better spot than
One Club; but if you disturb One Club you will not be able to stop just
where you want.

On (ii) it is wise to pass One Spade but permissible to respond One Heart
to One Diamond since it does not raise the level of the contract and gives
partner a chance to show a second suit, One No-Trump is the standard
response on hands that contain about 6–9 points and no suit that can be
bid at the level of One.

(iii) ♠ K 10 8   (iv) ♠ K 10 7
   ♡ 5 3   ♡ Q 8 4
   ◇ A 7 6 4   ◇ J 6 4 2
   ♣ Q 8 3 2   ♣ 7 5 3

Hand (iii) is close to a maximum for a response of One No-Trump to One Heart. Hand (iv) is close to a minimum.

(v) ♠ 7   (vi) ♠ 9 5
   ♡ Q 10 8 6 3   ♡ 2
   ◇ K 9 6 4   ◇ Q 10 7 6 3 2
   ♣ K 5 2   ♣ A 9 6 4

On hand (v) the response to One Club or One Diamond would be One Heart (though Two Diamonds over One Diamond would not be wrong); but over One Spade the response must be One No-Trump, for the hand does not qualify for a response at the two level.

Example (vi), in response to One Heart, is an awkward hand of a type that is seldom found in the text-books but often comes up at the table. The 6-4-2-1 distribution is unsuitable for One No-Trump; the hand is well below strength for a response of Two Diamonds; you could 'take a view' and pass, but that might be wrong also if partner had a big hand with some support for diamonds. In practice, most good players would respond One No-Trump despite the shape.

Raising partner's suit

When partner has opened with a major suit, especially, the best response, if the values are there, is usually an immediate raise of his suit. The first requirement is adequate trump support. Since players commonly open on four-card suits it is desirable to have four trumps for any jump raise, but a single raise can be freely given on three trumps headed by an honour. Except in rare occasions when an intervening bid has prevented the normal response, it is never right to support immediately on two trumps, even though they be ace-king. It is true that in that event, partner is likely to have a five-card suit, but some other response should be available on the first round.

In assessing the value of a hand for a raise of partner's suit, ruffing values (that is, short suits in conjunction with good trumps) have to be taken into account as much as high cards. A single raise shows about 6–9 points and a ruffing value. However, we shall find in the examples that follow that many more factors enter than can be contained in any short guide.

(i) ♠ K 10 8 6   (ii) ♠ A 10 8 4
     ♡ 5 3   ♡ K 8 2
     ◇ K 9 5   ◇ Q 7 6 3
     ♣ J 7 4 3   ♣ 10 5

Hand (i) is a weak raise of One Spade to Two Spades. Over One Diamond or One Heart, a one-over-one response of One Spade is best. Over One Club, since the hand is worth only one call, a raise to Two Clubs is rather better than One Spade.

Hand (ii) is a strong raise of One Spade to Two Spades. Over One Heart, a raise to Two Hearts is best. Here the principle is that when a hand is worth only one call preference should be given to the raise of partner's major suit. Over One Diamond, a raise to Two Diamonds would not be a mistake, but since the hand may well finish in no-trumps the more constructive response of One Spade is in order. Over One Club, either One Diamond or One Spade could be bid.

(iii) ♠ Q 8 6 4 3   (iv) ♠ Q 7 6
       ♡ 3   ♡ K J 4
       ◇ 10 7 4 2   ◇ K 7 6 2
       ♣ J 9 5   ♣ J 10 5

Although hand (iii) possesses only 3 points, it is perfectly correct to raise One Spade to Two Spades. Even if the values were not there it would be right to support for defensive reasons – to make it more difficult for the enemy to intervene in hearts. For the same sort of reason it would not be wrong, especially not vulnerable against vulnerable opponents, to raise an opening One Diamond. If nothing better, the raise might prepare for a profitable sacrifice at a high level.

Hand (iv) is an uncomfortable type that is strong for One No-Trump and weak, as we shall see shortly, for Two No-Trumps. A raise of One Spade to Two Spades, or of One Heart to Two Hearts, is the solution generally found. Over One Club or One Diamond, a response of One No-Trump is more acceptable, for the limits of a One No-Trump response to a minor are slightly higher than in response to a major.

For a double raise, an approximate standard is about 10–11 points with a doubleton and four trumps; but here, again, good distributional values may compensate for lack of high cards.

(v) ♠ 7 4   (vi) ♠ J 10 7 3
     ♡ K Q 6 2   ♡ 4
     ◇ K J 9 3   ◇ K 10 7 5 3
     ♣ K 10 5   ♣ A 6 2

Hand (v) is a solid raise of One Heart to Three Hearts. The values are also there for a double raise of an opening One Diamond, but since the hand is well suited for play in no-trumps it would be better to make an approach bid of One Heart; diamond support can be shown later.

On hand (vi) it would probably do no harm to respond Two Diamonds over One Spade, but a direct raise to Three Spades is preferable. Over One Diamond raise to Three Diamonds, for this hand is not so well adapted to play in no-trumps.

A triple raise, from One to Four, is treated by some players as a natural 'value' call, by others as primarily a shut-out or 'pre-emptive' bid.

(vii) ♠ –	(viii) ♠ A 8
♡ Q 10 8 7 4	♡ K 9 6 4
◇ K J 9 6 5 3	◇ A 10 3
♣ 10 2	♣ K 6 4 2

The pre-emptive school would raise One Heart to Four Hearts on (vii). On (viii), which is a strong raise to Four Hearts and a hand of different character, they would make some temporising bid such as Two Clubs and raise to Four Hearts on the next round, thus distinguishing between the two types of hand. There is no need to fall decisively on either side of this theoretical fence, for no calamity will ensue if Four Hearts is bid equally on both hands.

A raise to Four or Five in a minor is comparatively rare. It shows a hand with strong distributional support on which no contract has to be considered apart from the suit that partner has opened.

Responses of Two No-Trumps and Three No-Trumps

Two No-Trumps is a very common and useful response on balanced hands with about 11–12 points.

(i) ♠ Q 10 7 2	(ii) ♠ K 6
♡ K 9 4	♡ A 10 5
◇ A 10 8	◇ K 10 7 4 2
♣ K 6 4	♣ Q 9 4

Hand (i) is a typical Two No-Trump response to One Heart, One Diamond or One Club. Over One Spade, Three Spades would be in order.

On (ii) it would not be wrong to respond Two Diamonds to One Spade, but it is often a good tactical move to suppress the five-card suit and Two No-Trumps is the bid that most good players would make. Similarly, over One Club, One Diamond would be orthodox, but Two No-Trumps must be as good. Over One Diamond, 2NT is certainly best. Over One Heart, Two No-Trumps might turn out well but Two Diamonds is sounder because the hand may play better in hearts: you don't want to 'shut out' your own side.

Three No-Trumps, showing about 13–15 points, is a much less respected figure in the list of responses. It is a difficult bid over which to move should there be prospects of a slam, and should partner have a second suit he cannot show it without going beyond the Three No-Trump level. Consequently, on most hands that fall within the 13–15 range it is better to begin with a simple response in another suit; Three No-Trumps can always follow. An immediate Three No-Trumps is in order on a flat 4-3-3-3 and is sometimes a fair tactical bid on a 5-3-3-2 distribution.

(iii)	♠ K J 4	(iv)	♠ K 3
	♡ 10 6 3 2		♡ K 10 4
	◇ A Q 9		◇ A J 10 7 3
	♣ K Q 6		♣ Q J 6

On (iii) Three No-Trumps could be bid over any opening of One. On (iv) there is nothing better in response to One Diamond and it would not be a bad bid over One Spade.

It will be noted that these responses of Two No-Trumps and Three No-Trumps are not made with a singleton of partner's suit. A non-systematic player will tend to make the wrong bid on a hand such as:

♠ Q 10 8 3
♡ 5
◇ A Q J 4
♣ K J 10 3

In response to partner's One Heart opening, he is apt to say to himself: 'I have the other suits sewn up: "Three No-Trumps!"'

That may pass off all right, but there are two disadvantages to the bid: firstly, some delicate bidding may be needed to pave the way to a slam contract in one of the other three suits; secondly, the opening bidder, having a singleton somewhere, may go back to Four Hearts and be disappointed in the trump holding opposite. In other words, Two No-Trumps and Three No-Trumps are in no sense 'denial' bids so far as partner's suit is concerned. On the hand above it is better to make an approach bid of One Spade or Two Clubs. If partner just repeats his hearts you can bid Three No-Trumps on the next round, and if partner then goes to Four Hearts it will be his affair.

Responding at the level of two

It has already been noted, in passing, that a response of Two in a suit shows better than a minimum hand. As a rule, the bid promises about 9 points, but this may be less when a strong suit is held.

(i)   ♠ 7 4   (ii)   ♠ 7 4
      ♡ Q J 10 7 5   ♡ Q J 10 7 5 2
      ◇ K 8 6 4   ◇ K 8 6 4
      ♣ J 3   ♣ 3

On (i) the correct response to One Spade is One No-Trump. On (ii) the length and strength of the heart suit makes Two Hearts the only sensible call, but in any subsequent bidding responder must bear in mind that he has given a misleading impression of his high-card strength.

The suit itself does not have to be strong for a response at the two level.

(iii)   ♠ A K 4   (iv)   ♠ 4
       ♡ 6 3   ♡ A J 6 3
       ◇ A 8 7 2   ◇ K 10 8 5
       ♣ K J 6 3   ♣ Q 9 7 4

On (iii) the best response to One Heart is Two Clubs. Over One Spade, also, it is not wrong to approach with Two Clubs, though now the hand almost justifies a jump to Three Clubs.

On (iv) it would be a mistake to respond Two Hearts to One Spade because this promises a five-card suit. In any case, Two Clubs, leaving more room for development, is rather better. It will be noted that in responding the lower-ranked suit is often preferred when both are of four cards; as between two five-card suits it is usual to bid the higher-ranking, and when suits are of unequal length, the longer first.

Forcing responses

Although a simple response in a new suit is forcing for one round, on very strong hands it saves time in the end to signal the strength at once with a jump bid, such as Two Hearts over One Club, or Three Diamonds over One Spade. Such bids are unconditionally forcing on both partners until game (or a profitable double) is reached. That is why these bids in fact save time: once there has been a force, both partners can make bids at a minimum level with no fear of the bidding 'dying'.

It is usually in order to force at the level of Two with a fair suit to call, some support for partner, and about 15 points. A force at the level of Three should be slightly stronger. Good values in any one department – a suit of one's own, excellent support for partner, high cards – will compensate for deficiency in another.

(i) ♠ 6 4
     ♡ K Q 10 8 7 6
     ◇ A J 5
     ♣ A 3

(ii) ♠ 7
      ♡ K Q 6 2
      ◇ A K 10 6 5
      ♣ J 10 7

Hand (i), with the strong suit and good controls, is worth Two Hearts over One Diamond or One Club. Over One Spade, Two Hearts is sufficient.

On (ii) it would be right to force with Three Diamonds over One Heart or with Two Hearts over One Diamond. Over One Spade or One Club, make a simple response in diamonds; you will go to game eventually but the intention to go to game does not of itself justify an immediate force.

(iii) ♠ A Q 10 7 5 3
       ♡ K J 9 6 2
       ◇ J 4
       ♣ –

(iv) ♠ K 7 5 2
      ♡ A Q J 3
      ◇ Q 5
      ♣ A J 4

On (iii) respond simply One Spade to One Diamond or One Club. You do not have to jump on the first round in order to insist on game. Over One Heart, force with Two Spades; the distribution is so powerful that you want to give partner every encouragement to show his controls.

On (iv) you would probably land on your feet if you jumped straight to Six Hearts over One Heart, but the orthodox procedure is to force with Three Clubs. That is better than introducing an element of uncertainty by bidding the moderate spades; if partner raises clubs, a lower-ranking suit, you can always return to hearts.

Pre-emptive responses

Since the jump in a new suit is unlimited in strength, a response at a higher level is pre-emptive in character: it shows a hand that is weak in high cards and will play well only in the suit named.

(i) ♠ K Q J 9 7 6 4 2
     ♡ 3
     ◇ J 10 5
     ♣ 4

(ii) ♠ 7
      ♡ A J 10 9 6 5 4
      ◇ 4 2
      ♣ J 7 6

Hand (i) justifies a response of Four Spades to any opening bid of One. On (ii) Three Hearts could be bid over One Diamond or One Club. Over One Spade the response must be Two Hearts.

Responding after a pass

When a player has passed originally and his partner has opened in third or fourth seat, a simple response in a new suit is no longer forcing. The effect of this is that delicate approach bids by the responder should be forsworn in favour of direct action more likely to produce, if not a game, at any rate a plus score.

(i)	♠ Q 6 3		(ii)	♠ A Q 6 4 2
	♡ J 7 4 2			♡ 3
	◇ A J 7 5			◇ K 10 6 4
	♣ K 10			♣ Q 8 5

On (i) the normal response to One Spade is an exploratory Two Diamonds. That would not be good if you had previously passed, however, for it might be left in. The alternatives, though neither call is ideal, are Two No-Trumps or Three Spades.

Hand (ii), following an original pass, calls for a jump to Two Spades after partner has opened One Diamond. This jump should be understood by him as forcing for at least one round but it is not unconditionally forcing to game.

Over One Club or One Heart it is sufficient to bid simply One Spade. Game is not likely unless partner can bid once again, as he will if he had other than a completely minimum opening. It is a mistake to bid Two Spades simply to show that you had a good pass.

It is also a mistake to overbid in no-trumps because you have passed originally, bidding Three No-Trumps when your hand is worth only Two. The fact that you have passed originally doesn't make your hand any stronger – a truism that many players fail to recognise throughout their bridge career.

When there has been an intervening bid

When partner's opening is overcalled by the next player, lack of bidding space will often prevent responder from making his natural call.

(i)	♠ 6 4		(ii)	♠ 9 5 3
	♡ K 10 7 5 3			♡ 10 6 4
	◇ J 4			◇ A 8 6 2
	♣ K 8 6 2			♣ K Q 9

On (i) you would respond One Heart to One Diamond, but if second hand has overcalled with One Spade you can only pass: it would be very unsound to bid at the level of Two, especially in a straggly suit of higher rank than partner's.

On (ii), if partner opens One Spade and second hand intervenes with Two Hearts, you cannot consider Three Diamonds. You must either pass or bid Two Spades, despite the moderate trumps and absence of ruffing values.

In general, these so-called 'free' responses suggest better than a minimum. The range for a response of One No-Trump, in particular, is higher than when this bid is made to give partner another chance.

<table>
<tr><td>(iii)</td><td>♠ K 10 5</td><td>(iv)</td><td>♠ K 7 3</td></tr>
<tr><td></td><td>♡ 7 6 3</td><td></td><td>♡ J 10 7 5</td></tr>
<tr><td></td><td>◇ A 8 4</td><td></td><td>◇ 6 2</td></tr>
<tr><td></td><td>♣ Q J 8 2</td><td></td><td>♣ Q 7 5 4</td></tr>
</table>

After 1◇ – 1♠, the bid on (iii) is One No-Trump. Had second hand overcalled with One Heart, One No-Trump would be ruled out through lack of a guard in hearts; the bid would be Two Clubs.

On (iv), after 1◇ – 1♡ (or 1♠), responder should pass rather than make a free bid of One No-Trump. Responder should also pass after 1♠ – 2◇.

Many players, including all who play in the American style, would say that responder should pass after 1♡ – 2◇. But here, while you are technically short of the values for a free raise, I advise competing at a low level while you can.

Responses after a double by second hand are based on different principles altogether; they are described in Chapter 10.

6

No-Trump Bids and Responses

No-trump bidding is complicated by the fact that there are several different theories about the standard to adopt for an opening One No-Trump. So there are about most things in bridge, to be sure, but One No-Trump is such a common opening that it is necessary to remark on the principal variations.

There are, as a matter of fact, two general types of One No-Trump opening:

A weak no-trump of 12–14 points

A strong no-trump of 15–17 points

Some think vulnerability is an important factor because an opening One No-Trump, showing a fair balanced hand, is exposed to a much keener wind, should partner be weak, than an opening bid in a suit. It is far easier for the opponents, when they hold the balance of the cards, to align their forces for a double of One No-Trump than for a double of a suit contract. Some of these players like to play a variable no-trump, 12–14 when non-vulnerable and 15–17 vulnerable. The problem with this idea is that it means that there are two different systems to be learned and for most people bridge is difficult enough with only one. So we will concentrate on those situations where the opening no-trump is 12-14 points.

Modern philosophy is that all balanced hands should either open One No-Trump or rebid in no-trumps at the first opportunity (unless a 4-4 major-suit fit has been found).

Opening a weak no-trump

The following would be good examples of a weak no-trump:

(i) ♠ K 9 4   (ii) ♠ A 4
     ♡ Q 10 7 3   ♡ K 10 8 5
     ◇ K J 4   ◇ 6 4 3
     ♣ A J 7   ♣ A Q 7 2

Raises of One No-Trump

To value a hand for a raise of partner's One No-Trump opening, it is helpful to keep in mind that on balanced hands a combined count of 25 points will generally provide a play for game. The standard for a single raise of a weak no-trump is 11–12 points.

(i) ♠ A 6 4   (ii) ♠ A J 9
     ♡ K Q 3   ♡ Q 10 7 4
     ◇ J 6 4 2   ◇ K 6
     ♣ J 5 2   ♣ J 10 8 3

Hand (i) would be described as a 'bad 11', for there are no intermediates and the distribution is the unproductive 4-3-3-3. It is not worth a raise of a One No-Trump to Two.

Hand (ii) is a 'good 11'. The two tens, especially in conjunction with higher honours, are worth at least 1 point, and it would not be overbold to raise One No-Trump to Three.

The next two examples show that a long suit does not preclude a raise of the no-trump opening.

(iii) ♠ 6 2   (iv) ♠ K 7 4
       ♡ K Q 7 4 3   ♡ J 6 3
       ◇ A 10 5   ◇ A Q 7 5 3 2
       ♣ Q 6 3   ♣ 5

On (iii) it is so unlikely that you would make Four Hearts and not Three No-Trumps that the natural response to One No-Trump is Three No-Trumps. On (iv) the bid is Three No-Trumps, for you are likely to make about seven tricks or ten, according to whether or not you can bring in the diamonds quickly. On such a hand you do not want to languish in Two No-Trumps; nor should you want to attempt Five Diamonds.

A player who has opened One No-Trump and been raised to Two should bid game unless his opening was a minimum; raises to Two are calculated on that basis.

Suit responses to One No-Trump

The system we shall recommend here is that a simple take-out should be discouraging. The opener will usually pass the response, but may raise with a maximum and good support.

(i)   ♠ Q 9 7 6 4   (ii)   ♠ 7 3
      ♡ 2   ♡ K J 8 4 2
      ◇ J 8 5   ◇ A 10 9 6
      ♣ 9 6 4 2   ♣ 7 5

Bid Two Spades on hand (i) and Two Hearts on (ii).

A jump to Three of a suit is forcing in all standard systems.

(iii)   ♠ K 5   (iv)   ♠ A 8 4
       ♡ A J 4 3   ♡ Q 10 7 6 4
       ◇ A 10   ◇ K Q 6 2
       ♣ A K 6 4 2   ♣ 4

With 19 points, there are slam prospects on hand (iii). Bid Three Clubs. Partner will bid a four-card heart suit if he has one. Even though hand (iv) is much weaker, you should still jump to Three Hearts. If partner rebids Three No-Trumps, you should pass. Don't worry about your singleton club; it is more than likely that he is strong in that suit.

Opening bids of Two No-Trumps and responses

The standard strength for a Two No-Trump opening is 20–22 points.

(i)   ♠ K J 4   (ii)   ♠ K 6 4
      ♡ A K 10 5   ♡ A J 3
      ◇ K Q 8 3   ◇ A K Q 10 7
      ♣ A Q   ♣ K 7

Although hand (i) has two fair suits and a doubleton, the honour strength is such that Two No-Trumps is a better opening than One Heart. On (ii) Two No-Trumps is a better tactical opening than One Diamond. Should you open One Diamond and partner respond One No-Trump the disadvantage will follow that the opening lead will come through your strong hand. Moreover, as a general principle, it is better that the strong hand should be concealed than be exposed on the table.

Responder should raise Two No-Trumps to Three on about 4½ points – less if he has a playable five-card suit. Any suit response at the level of Three is forcing, though it does not have to be strong. A jump to game, 2NT – 4♡, is best played as a slam suggestion.

Opening bids of Three No-Trumps and responses

Given that all hands that are very strong in terms of high cards are opened with Two Clubs, it is sensible to use Three No-Trumps as a tactical opening bid on a hand containing a long minor suit.

	(i)		(ii)	
	♠	Q 4	♠	K Q 7
	♡	A 10	♡	A K J 5
	◇	A K Q 10 7 5 3	◇	A Q 10
	♣	K J	♣	A Q J

Three No-Trumps is a good opening on (i). It is clear that to make Three No-Trumps you need less from partner than you do for Five Diamonds. Knowing the type of hand, partner will not take out into, say, Four Spades because he has K-x-x-x-x of spades and little else.

On a hand with genuine no-trump shape, such as (ii), the first bid should be a conventional Two Clubs, with Three No-Trumps as the rebid.

Any response to a Three No-Trump opening, whether or not preceded by Two Clubs, is constructive: that is to say, responder is not called upon to rescue on a weak hand.

Nowadays, many tournament players take this principle of opening Three No-Trumps on a long minor suit a stage further. They would use it to show a solid minor suit with little at all outside. If partner has some values in the outside suits he passes, while with a weak hand he removes to Four of a minor, making it very difficult for his opponents to find their best spot.

7

Bidding to Partscore and Game

The last three chapters have set out the groundwork of constructive bidding. Before passing on to the next stage – opening bids of more than One, defensive bidding, slam bidding and the like – it may be well to stop for some practical exercises in partnership bidding. Otherwise, the game will begin to wear too theoretical an aspect. At the same time we shall encounter many new words and conventions that are part of the language of bidding.

In all the following examples West is the dealer and the score is Love All.

Trial bids by opener

```
♠ A Q 10 5 3        ┌─────────┐        ♠ J 9 6 4
♡ J                 │    N    │        ♡ Q 8 3 2
♢ A 8 6 2           │ W     E │        ♢ K 7
♣ K Q 5             │    S    │        ♣ J 8 3
                    └─────────┘
```

The bidding goes:

West	East
1♠	2♠
3♢(1)	4♠(2)
Pass	

(1) After the raise West has enough to try for game. How does he know that? Well, certain forms of point count have been devised for this and most other basic situations, but good players do not use them. Such hands are so common that one soon learns to assess them at sight. Until that kind of judgement has been developed, these are two tests that can be applied:

Speaking very generally, after a single raise in a major the opener requires two full playing tricks more than his opening bid to be in the game zone. West has that here: he has at least a queen more than is needed in terms of high cards, he has a good trump suit of five cards, and he has the beginnings of a second suit. A hand with 5-4-3-1 distribution is decidedly stronger than one with 5-3-3-2.

Another rough way of judging whether the hand is worth a game try is to ascribe average values to partner and mentally put the two hands together. Suppose, here, that you imagine partner to have an ace and a king: added to West's hand, that should be enough.

The next question, then, is what West should bid. It would not be unduly rash to go straight to Four Spades; many players would do that. A simple bid of Three Spades would not be sufficiently encouraging. Better is to make what is known as a 'trial bid' in another suit. The natural choice here is Three Diamonds. That change of suit after a raise is unconditionally forcing: it many not show a suit of any length at all, so in no circumstances must responder (supposing that he has better support for the second suit than for the first) say, 'No bid.'

(2) Now East has to decide whether to bid Three Spades, warning partner not to continue, or Four Spades. It may seem that East has a weak raise and must sign off. However, partner would not make the trial bid unless he had high hopes of game, and East should say to himself not, 'Am I strong?' but 'Am I as bad as I might be?' The answer to that is, 'No', for East has fairly good trumps and moreover he has a useful holding in diamonds, the suit that partner has bid. One of the objects of a trial bid is to direct partner's attention to a suit in which support would be welcome. So, East is able to venture Four Spades.

In the play West will aim to ruff two diamonds and should succeed for the loss of a heart, a club, and probably a trump.

A jump rebid of Two No-Trumps and a jump to game by responder

♠ A J
♡ A Q 10
◇ Q J 9 7 6
♣ K 8 4

♠ Q 10 8 7 6 4
♡ J 8 5 3
◇ 6
♣ A 5

The bidding goes:

West	East
1◇	1♠
2NT(1)	4♠(2)
Pass	

(1) Since a partner who responds at the level of One may have a minimum hand, perhaps only 5 or 6 points, the opener must be strong to jump to Two No-Trumps. The usual standard is 17–18 or 19 points.

(2) A simple rebid of his own suit by responder over Two No-Trumps would be a sign-off and would be passed by opener. Consequently, East must jump to game with Four Spades. The 7 points that he can contribute to his partner's 17 puts him in the game zone and naturally he prefers to play in a spade contract. Three No-Trumps could easily fail on a club lead.

A reverse by opener and a limit bid by responder

♠ A 4
♡ 7 3
♢ A Q 10 6
♣ K Q J 5 3

♠ J 6 2
♡ K J 9 6 5 2
♢ 8 3
♣ 7 4

The bidding goes:

West	East
1♣	1♡
2♢(1)	2♡(2)
Pass(3)	

(1) With 16 HCP West's choices of rebid lie between One No-Trump to show a balanced 15–17 points, and a reverse into his second suit. With such good suits, West chooses the latter action. This reverse is forcing for one round.

(2) By simply rebidding his hearts at minimum level East makes about the weakest bid open to him. Also limited would be a simple return to Three Clubs. With the king of spades instead of a small one, East would bid Two No-Trumps rather than Two Hearts.

(3) Having little in reserve, considering that he has already made a reverse bid, and recognising that partner is strictly limited, West shows good judgement in passing Two Hearts.

A jump rebid by responder

♠ 9 5
♡ K Q 5
♢ A K 10 7 6 4
♣ 6 2

♠ K Q 10 8 6 4
♡ 7 3
♢ 5 2
♣ A J 4

The bidding goes:

West	East
1♦	1♠
2♦	3♠(1)
4♠(2)	Pass

(1) Although partner has made a comparatively weak rebid, East can make this strong try for game. One way of arriving at that conclusion is for East to note that his own hand has the values for an opening bid, albeit a minimum. It is a sound proposition that when the two hands contain between them the values for two opening bids a game should be possible so long as there be some declaration suitable to both hands. If only because of the latter provision East cannot jump to Four Spades, but he can invite game with a jump to Three.

(2) West can bid the game because, having regard to the fact that so far he has only bid and rebid diamonds, he is by no means unsuitable for a spade contract: he has two trumps, a doubleton and three quick tricks.

Bidding a short suit at the level of three

♠ K 10　　　　　　　　♠ 6 3 2
♡ A K J 7 4 2　　　　♡ 5
♦ 10 4　　　　　　　　♦ A Q J 9 6 3
♣ J 4 2　　　　　　　　♣ A Q 3

The bidding goes:

West	East
1♡	2♦
2♡	3♣(1)
3NT(2)	Pass

(1) As in the previous example, East has the values for an opening bid himself and consequently looks for a game contract. Three Diamonds in this position would not be a weak call, for with a poor hand East would pass, but it would not be sufficiently strong. Four Diamonds would carry the partnership beyond the level of Three No-Trumps. The best solution is to 'invent' a bid of Three Clubs. As a general proposition, it may be taken that a new suit at the level of Three, introduced by either partner, is forcing for one round. Thus there is no danger that Three Clubs may be passed; if it is raised to Four, East can revert to Four Diamonds.

(2) If West had no guard in spades, the unbid suit, he would have to bid Three Hearts or Three Diamonds. As it is, he is reasonably happy to bid

Three No-Trumps. This can fail if spades are led and the diamond finesse is wrong, but game is always worth bidding on an even chance.

Stopping with a misfit

```
♠ J                          ♠ A Q 8 6 3
♡ K Q 8 6 3 2     N          ♡ 4
◇ 7            W     E        ◇ K Q 8 5 4
♣ A J 9 5 4        S          ♣ 7 2
```

The bidding goes:

West	East
1♡	1♠
2♣	2◇
2♡	Pass (1)

(1) This is the sort of pass, it must be said, that only a good player would make. Yet it should be clear to East that prospects of game are most uncertain: partner is marked with at least ten cards in hearts and clubs, nor are there grounds for supposing that he has more than a minimum in high cards. A further point is that even if there should be a game contract in some denomination it will not be easy to alight in the best spot. Thus, the sensible course is to drop the bidding. It is the sort of hand on which two pig-headed players would battle against one another till they lost 500 in some contract like Four Clubs doubled.

Jump preference by responder

```
♠ 6 3                        ♠ A K 8 4 2
♡ K Q 10 7 5      N          ♡ 6 4 2
◇ A Q 9 5 2    W     E        ◇ K 7 4
♣ J               S          ♣ 10 6
```

The bidding goes:

West	East
1♡	1♠
2◇	3♡(1)
4♡(2)	Pass

(1) If East were weaker say, without the king of spades – he would give simple preference with Two Hearts. As it is, he must take stronger action, and despite the indifferent trumps the jump preference in hearts is by far the best call. An immediate jump raise, 1♡ – 3♡, would naturally promise better trump support, but here the fact that West has bid his hand as a two-suiter gives ground for supposing that his suits are fairly good.

East has the values also for a raise to Three Diamonds, but the fact that he has the king of this suit and not of hearts is beside the point. As on the actual hand, ten tricks may well be easier to make in hearts than in diamonds. In any case, it is sensible to play for game in the major.

(2) West has not much more than he has already shown, but his strength seems to be in the right place. It is a recommendation that his doubleton is in his partner's suit and his singleton in the unbid suit where probably both players are weak.

8

Opening Bids of More than One

Opening bids of Two can be, and are, put to various uses. In the early days of contract bridge, the 'Forcing Two' of the Culbertson system was standard practice. More common in Britain (and demonstrably superior) are the Two Club systems in which very strong hands are opened with a conventional bid of Two Clubs that does not show clubs at all. Two bids of the other suits can be played as forcing for one round, as strong but not forcing, or even, as is increasingly common these days, as very weak indeed, designed mainly to make life difficult for opponents.

The simplest system to play, especially with a strange partner, is that in which Two bids are strong but only forcing for one round. That is the method we shall recommend here.

Opening Two bids and responses

The main reason for opening with a Two bid is to extract a response from a partner who might have to pass a bid of One. At the same time, it is often an advantage to communicate a very powerful hand in one bid. These are some borderline examples:

(i)	♠ 5 4		(ii)	♠ A J
	♡ A Q 10 9 6 4			♡ A Q 7 5 4
	◇ A K Q 7			◇ J 2
	♣ 3			♣ A K 7 3

Hand (i) is powerful but not of sufficient quality to warrant a Two Heart opening. Since you have only 15 points it is not likely that One Heart will be passed out: even if partner cannot respond, the opponents will probably have something to say.

Hand (ii) is stronger in terms of points but has only a five-card suit and is not so powerful as to demand a Two opening. If partner cannot respond to One Heart, game is unlikely; if he does respond, you force with Three Clubs on the next round.

(iii) ♠ K Q J 9 7 6   (iv) ♠ 5
    ♡ A 4   ♡ A K 10 9 5
    ◇ A K 3   ◇ A K 7 4 2
    ♣ 6 2   ♣ A 3

Hand (iii) qualifies for an opening of Two Spades. If partner responds Two No-Trumps, which can be quite weak, the rebid is simply Three Spades, which partner can pass if he has a singleton spade and no ace or king. If the opener were stronger – say with the jack of diamonds instead of a small club – he would go to Four Spades over the Two No-Trump response.

Hand (iv), though it contains five quick tricks and two good suits, is just not solid enough for a game-forcing opening of Two Clubs. Two Hearts is sufficient.

The responder is not allowed to pass with a valueless hand and no support for opener. On all hands of little or moderate strength his first response should be Two No-Trumps.

(v) ♠ 7 4   (vi) ♠ Q 10 8 6 3
  ♡ Q 10 6 3   ♡ 5 2
  ◇ J 9 5 2   ◇ K 9 4 3
  ♣ 6 4 3   ♣ 7 4

Hand (v) just warrants a response of Two No-Trumps to Two Spades. If partner rebids Three Spades you can pass. If he rebids in either of the red suits you can raise. A rebid of Three Clubs would present you with a close decision, whether to pass or take a chance on Three No-Trumps.

If partner were to open Two Hearts, your first response on this hand should be the warning Two No-Trumps. You can go to game in hearts on the next round.

Similarly, on hand (vi), the response to Two Hearts should be Two No-Trumps, not Two Spades. If partner were to open Two Spades you might respond Four Spades. It is a matter for partnership agreement, but it is sensible to use that double raise to show a hand with good trumps and little else.

On stronger hands the bidding should be allowed to develop at an even pace: there is seldom need for either player to jump.

(vii) ♠ 10 4   (viii)♠ A K Q J 7 3
　　♡ K J 8 5   　　♡ 5 2
　　◇ A 10 6 2   　　◇ 7 6 3
　　♣ J 6 4   　　♣ 9 5

On hand (vii) simply respond Three No-Trumps to an opening of Two Spades. This bid suggests about 8-11 points distributed over the other three suits.

If partner were to open Two Hearts the best response would be a simple Three Hearts. That sets the suit and leaves room for exchange of information. Any positive response – that is, any response other than Two No-Trumps – is forcing to game.

Hand (viii) is the rare type on which a jump is recommended. Over Two Hearts or Two Diamonds (also over Two Clubs, when we come to that) jump to Three Spades. That is a useful convention to show a solid suit for which no support is required.

Opening bid of Two Clubs and responses

An opening bid of Two Clubs (in the system as is presented here) denotes a game-going hand. It is not necessary to see a certain game in one's own hand but the opener must be prepared to play in game even if his partner is very weak.

The only time when the partnership may stop short of game is when the bidding goes: 2♣ – 2◇ (weakness response) – 2NT. Even then it is a debatable point – a matter for agreement between partners – whether responder should be allowed to pass on a hand containing fewer than 3 points. On the whole, to make the sequence non-forcing extends the range and accuracy of no-trump bidding, and we shall recommend that here.

A Two Club opening should normally contain upwards of 23 high-card points. There are, however, some exceptionally powerful hands, generally two-suiters, on which the bid has to be made on rather less.

(i) ♠ A Q   (ii) ♠ A K J 9 3
　　♡ A K Q 10 4   ♡ A Q J 7 6 4
　　◇ K 7 3   ◇ –
　　♣ A J 9   ♣ A 5

The best way to bid hand (i) is to open Two Clubs and make the non-forcing rebid of Two No-Trumps. That way, you ensure that the lead in a no-trump contract will come up to the strong hand, with obvious advantage in this case. Partner will pass Two No-Trumps only if he has an almost worthless hand.

The fact that you have both majors justifies an opening of Two Clubs on hand (ii). Over partner's response first show hearts, the longer suit, and then spades.

As has already been remarked, the weakness response to Two Clubs is Two Diamonds. However weak responder may be, he must keep the bidding open to game except on the one occasion when partner rebids Two No-Trumps: then he can pass if he has no more than one queen.

There are no precise requirements for a positive response – any response, that is, other than the negative Two Diamonds.

(iii)	♠ 7 4 2	(iv)	♠ Q 10 6 2
	♡ 6 3		♡ K J 4
	♢ 10 7 4		♢ J 7 6
	♣ K 9 6 4 2		♣ K 6 2

On hand (iii) respond Two Diamonds on the first round and raise Two No-Trumps to Three. Should partner rebid Two Spades or Two Hearts, do not fear to show the clubs: you have already proclaimed that you have a poor hand.

Hand (iv) justifies a response of Two No-Trumps. If you do not make that response now it may be difficult later to give a picture of your scattered strength.

(v)	♠ Q 9 7 2	(vi)	♠ K J 10 7 4 3
	♡ 9 4 3		♡ 10
	♢ 6 2		♢ 8
	♣ A Q 6 4		♣ J 10 6 4 2

On hand (v) some players would respond Two No-Trumps, but it is better to show where the strength lies and bid Three Clubs.

Hand (vi) is potentially strong in playing tricks, but the first response should be Two Diamonds. Then you can make strong action later should it appear that partner has some fit for one of your suits.

Opening bids of Three and Four

Since every variety of strong hand can be shown by bids of One or Two, it follows that higher calls should be weaker in high cards and primarily defensive in purpose. They are known as pre-emptive bids.

The strength of these openings depends much on vulnerability and position at the table. Some players make a distinction between major and minor suits, but that is not general. The effect of these various considerations can best be explained by reference to particular hands.

(i) ♠ 4
     ♡ K Q J 10 6 4 3
     ◇ 7 5 2
     ♣ 9 6

(ii) ♠ K 10 7 4
      ♡ –
      ◇ Q J 10 7 6 5 2
      ♣ 8 6

Hand (i) is a typical Three Heart opening in any of the first three positions, not vulnerable. In third position, not vulnerable against vulnerable opponents, an aggressive player might open Four Hearts. The logical basis of such a call – in fact, of all pre-emptive bids – is that should you be doubled and go four down, making just six heart tricks, you will lose 800 (less 100 honours if playing rubber bridge) but will surely be saving a game, probably a slam. Vulnerable, the hand is a little under strength for an opening of Three, but the bid might be made third in hand at Game All.

Hand (ii) has the values for a pre-emptive Three Diamonds, so far as playing tricks go, but an objection to the call is that should partner have a strong hand, including a suit of spades, you will be shutting him out as much as the opponents. This objection would not exist if you were third to speak, and many players would then open Three Diamonds whether vulnerable or not. In practice, good players 'mix' their pre-emptive bids a good deal, sometimes slipping one in with more high-card points (especially facing a passed partner), sometimes making the bid on a two-suiter. At the rubber bridge table, especially when there is a partscore, it pays to keep opponents guessing.

(iii) ♠ A K Q 10 7 6 4 2
       ♡ 3
       ◇ J 7 2
       ♣ 5

(iv) ♠ 5
      ♡ A Q J 10 7 4 3
      ◇ Q J 8 6
      ♣ 5

Hand (iii) is a typical Four Spade opening in any position and at any score.

The bid on (iv) would depend on the score. Vulnerable against non-vulnerable, for example, you might open three Hearts; the other way round, Four Hearts. This is also the sort of hand, in so far as there is any standard type, on which you might open Three Hearts fourth in hand. You would hope to snatch a partscore should partner have his share of the outstanding strength, and since both opponents have passed you should not be unduly nervous of their bidding and making Four Spades.

Pre-emptive bids of Four and Five can also be made in minor suits.

(v) ♠ 7
     ♡ 10
     ◇ K Q J 10 8 6 5 4 2
     ♣ J 9 5

(vi) ♠ K J 9 3
      ♡ 10
      ◇ Q 7
      ♣ A K Q 7 6 5 3

With seven playing tricks and 100 honours, you could open Four Diamonds on (v). Hand (vi) contains some promise of game in no-trumps and to that extent is unsuitable for a pre-emptive bid, at any rate in first or second hand. So, the orthodox opening is One Club.

Responses to Three bids

When replying to his partner's pre-emptive bid, responder must study the score and other factors and consider whether partner is likely to be weak or relatively strong.

	(i)	♠ K 5 3	(ii)	♠ 7
		♡ 7 2		♡ K Q 4
		◇ A Q 6 4		◇ A Q 7 3
		♣ K J 8 5		♣ A Q 6 4 2

Hand (i) is of a type that will always deceive a beginner. It is a mistake to disturb an opening bid such as Three Hearts. If you put this hand opposite example (i) in the previous section, you will see that in combination they offer little or no prospect of either Three No-Trumps or Four Hearts.

Whether you should raise Three Spades to Four is close. If partner had opened Three Spades second in hand, vulnerable against non-vulnerable, you would raise; but if he had opened as dealer against vulnerable opponents you would be right to pass as often as not. These situations cannot be judged exactly, for much will depend on the exact distribution of partner's hand.

On (ii) the sensible call over Three Spades is Four Spades. It is true that if you bid Three No-Trumps most partners will go back to their own suit, but a good partner may assume that you have your reasons and pass. You should not want to play in no-trumps with a singleton of partner's suit, for there may well be a lack of entries to establish and run it.

A response of Four Clubs would be forcing and a slam suggestion, not justified on the present hand. In principle one does not fight partner's pre-emptive opening, except that a responder with a strong major suit may seek to play in that suit over partner's pre-empt in a minor. A sequence such as 3◇ – 3♡ is forcing. If the opener's hand is at all playable in hearts he should raise to Four.

9
The Defending Side

When a player opens the bidding he has a constructive purpose in view – to establish contact with partner and if possible to reach a game or slam. When a defender makes a simple overcall, on the other hand, his objective is not so much to arrive at a high contract as to harass the enemy. Playing strength now becomes more important than high-card points. For a simple overcall at the range of One, not vulnerable, a fair five-card suit and one honour trick will suffice.

(i)	♠ K Q 10 9 6	(ii)	♠ 7 4
	♡ 7 2		♡ A J 6 2
	◇ J 9 5 4		◇ Q 7 3
	♣ 8 3		♣ J 10 7 4

On hand (i) is it sound tactics to overcall One Club with One Spade. There is more sting to this bid than may appear at first sight. An overcall in spades, even at the one level, has a certain pre-emptive value, for it prevents the next player from making a one-over-one response. Third hand, in this instance, cannot respond One Heart or One Diamond and may have to pass through lack of a suitable call. Perhaps the other defender will be able to raise to Two Spades: then the defenders will be well on the way to stealing the contract with inferior cards.

A second advantage of the One Spade overcall is that it may deter the opponents from reaching Three No-Trumps. Even if they have the ace of spades they will not know that the player who has bid spades has no side entry.

Hand (ii) has much less to recommend it as an overcall of One Heart over One Club. In general, this is the sort of hand on which you should be more ready to defend than to contest, the more so as you have a trick in the suit that the opponent has called. The heart suit is poor and should the opponents buy the contract in no-trumps you do not want to encourage partner to lead hearts from a short suit. On this type of hand, therefore, it is better to pass.

(iii) ♠ 7 2
    ♡ A K 10 6 4
    ◇ K 5 3
    ♣ 6 4 2

(iv) ♠ K 6 3
    ♡ 8 5 4
    ◇ A Q J 9 6 2
    ♣ 7

On hand (iii) it is reasonable to overcall One Club or One Diamond with One Heart, but not good to overcall One Spade with Two Hearts. An overcall at the two level is much more likely to incur a penalty double and this hand contains too many losers.

Hand (iv) represents a minimum for a vulnerable overcall of Two Diamonds and even then you would run into an 800 penalty every so often. If the conditions are unfavourable – if you are vulnerable and they are not, and if partner has already passed – it is wiser not to overcall. You may have an opportunity to enter the bidding later after opponents have shown that they are limited in strength.

Take-out doubles

On stronger hands where a defender is ready to wage war for the contract rather than to engage in guerrilla activity, he will usually make what is known as a 'take-out' double. These doubles are especially useful when the defender is strong in all suits but the one opened.

(i) ♠ K J 9 4
    ♡ 3
    ◇ A 10 7 6 2
    ♣ K Q 6

(ii) ♠ K J 5
    ♡ A K J 7 4
    ◇ A 10 8
    ♣ Q 4

Hand (i) is exactly suited to a double of One Heart. It is not a good double of One Spade, however, for it lacks one of the chief requirements for a take-out double – namely, preparedness for any response. Partner's most likely response is in hearts and for that there is inadequate support; nor would it be profitable, opposite a moderate hand, to seek refuge in no-trumps. To overcall One Spade with Two Diamonds would also be misguided, for it might well lead to a penalty when there was nothing on for the opponents. The best plan is to pass One Spade; this is called a 'trap pass', for the object is to give rope to opponents who may be running into a misfit.

On hand (ii), although it contains a strong suit which you could safely call, it is best to double One Diamond or One Club. That is the proper bid on a hand with such good honour strength. You can show your hearts on the next round and partner will know that you have a hand of this sort.

Over One Spade you might overcall with One No-Trump if vulnerable; alternatively, a double would not be wrong. The action over One Heart would depend on the score. Not vulnerable against vulnerable you might make a trap pass, but if the score were the other way round it would be better to double and follow with a bid in no-trumps.

The take-out double is a flexible weapon for a player who has passed.

(iii) ♠ Q 8 5 4 2
  ♡ Q 10 8 6
  ♢ 3
  ♣ A J 4

(iv) ♠ K 10 8 4
  ♡ 7 3
  ♢ A J 9 5 2
  ♣ 10 4

Hand (iii) is too short of high cards for a double of One Diamond second in hand – 11 points is about the minimum even on such good distribution. But if you have passed originally and the bidding has been opened One Diamond by fourth hand you can show willingness to contest in any of the other suits by a second-round double.

Similarly, on hand (iv), if you pass as dealer, second hand opens One Club and fourth hand responds One Heart, you can show strength in the unbid suits by doubling at this point.

More about how a take-out double can be distinguished from a penalty double, and how take-out doubles can be used by the side that has opened the bidding, will be said in the next chapter. For the present we are concerned with the various ways in which the defending side can combat an adverse opening.

Responses to take-out doubles

At Game All the bidding begins:

South	West	North	East
1♡	Dble	Pass	?

The following are the main courses of action open to East, the doubler's partner:

1 With a weak, featureless hand, he must bid his best suit at the minimum level.

(i) ♠ 10 7 4
 ♡ J 8 5 2
 ♢ J 6 4 3
 ♣ 5 2

(ii) ♠ 8 6 4 2
  ♡ Q 7 6
  ♢ 6 3
  ♣ K 9 5 2

On (i) respond Two Diamonds. Things look bad, but partner is in control. It is a woeful error to pass on the grounds that it won't matter much if they make One Heart doubled. It will matter if they make several overtricks at 200 a time and partner will not forgive you if he has a strong spade suit which he was going to bid on the next round.

Had North, the opener's partner, made any bid, that would have created a different situation: with so poor a hand you should then pass.

On (ii), although the clubs are better than the spades, One Spade would be the normal response. In general, a player who doubles one major is expected to be strong in the other.

2   **With a stopper in the opponent's suit, East may respond in no-trumps.**

(iii) ♠ J 4   (iv) ♠ J 9
    ♡ K 10 7 3   ♡ A Q 6
    ♢ 7 6 4 2   ♢ K 10 7 4
    ♣ Q 5 2   ♣ 10 7 3 2

On hand (iii) the natural response in One No-Trump. This response promises slight values. If the present hand were weaker by a queen or so the right bid would be Two Diamonds.

Hand (iv), in conjunction with the vulnerable double, justifies a response of Two No-Trumps.

3   **With exceptional strength in the suit that has been doubled, East may pass, thus converting the take-out double into a penalty double.**

(v) ♠ Q 6   (vi) ♠ 6 4 2
  ♡ K J 9 7 3   ♡ Q J 10 9 7 6
  ♢ 7 4 2   ♢ J 3 2
  ♣ 10 5 2   ♣ 7

The trump holding in (v) is still not strong enough for a penalty pass. Sitting under the bidder, East will not be able to prevent declarer from making such trumps as he possesses. Respond One No-Trump.

Hand (vi) is the only type on which the penalty pass is in order. Note that the trumps are so strong that the defence can play trumps and draw those of declarer.

4   **With fair values, such as a five-card suit and 8–10 points, East should make a jump response.**

(vii) ♠ K J 8 7   (viii) ♠ 6 3
   ♡ 7 6 4   ♡ 7 6 4 2
   ♢ A 10 8 5   ♢ Q 2
   ♣ J 9   ♣ A K 8 6 3

Respond Two Spades on (vii) and Three Clubs on (viii). Whether these jump responses should be forcing for one round or just encouraging is a matter on which authorities disagree. Let us say that the doubler should not drop the bidding if his double was sound.

5   With a still stronger hand responder may either jump to game or make a forcing bid by calling the enemy suit.

(ix)   ♠ K J 8   (x)   ♠ A Q 10 7 6 4
       ♡ 6 4   ♡ 6 5 2
       ◇ A 10 7 3   ◇ A J 10
       ♣ K J 6 2   ♣ 6

On (ix) there must be a game somewhere and the best move is to put the ball back into partner's court by responding Two Hearts. This is forcing to game.

On (x) you could bid a direct Four Spades; but the way to show a hand that should be in the slam zone is to force with Two Hearts and then jump in spades.

Overcalling in no-trumps

An overcall of One No-Trump shows a hand of about 15–17 points not vulnerable, 17–18 vulnerable, with at least one stop in the opponent's suit.

(i)   ♠ Q J 7   (ii)   ♠ A 10 3
      ♡ K 6   ♡ K Q 7
      ◇ A K Q 7 3   ◇ K J 9 6
      ♣ J 5 2   ♣ K Q 4

On (i) One No-Trump, not vulnerable, is a good tactical overcall of One Heart or One Spade.

On (ii) One No-Trump is the natural vulnerable overcall of any One bid. Not vulnerable, the hand is a little strong: you can double first and bid no-trumps on the next round.

Jump overcalls

A jump overcall is an overcall one level higher than necessary, such as Two Hearts over One Club, or Three Clubs over One Diamond. It shows a good hand with the strength concentrated in one or sometimes two suits.

(i)   ♠ 7   (ii)   ♠ A K 10 7 6
      ♡ A K J 10 6 5   ♡ —
      ◇ A Q 8 4   ◇ A Q J 9 6 4
      ♣ 3 2   ♣ J 2

On (i) Two Hearts is the best bid over One Diamond or One Club. Over One Spade, either a double or Three Hearts is acceptable.

The jump overcall can also be made on a two-suiter such as (ii). Because of the shortage of hearts you cannot properly double One Club; the natural bid is Two Diamonds. Over One Heart you have a choice of bids, none of them ideal. Since you want to show your own suits rather than extract information from partner, a take-out double can be time-wasting, especially if the next opponent is able to pre-empt in hearts. Three Diamonds would not be wrong; but many players would make the quieter bid of One Spade, keeping the bidding low so as to give the other players a chance to call.

Jump overcalls are not forcing on partner but should be kept open on moderate values such as 8 or 9 points. Since the suit must be good, very little is required in the way of trump support.

Game-forcing overcalls

The strongest overcall is a bid of the opponent's sit. As a rule this shows first-round control of that suit as well as a very powerful hand.

(i) ♠ K Q 10 6   (ii) ♠ A Q J 9 6 4
     ♡ A K J 9 5   ♡ 4
     ◇ −   ◇ A K 10 7 6 3
     ♣ A Q J 4   ♣ −

Hand (i), a giant take-out double of One Diamond, calls rather for the immediate overcall of Two Diamonds. On (ii) bid Two Clubs over One Club or Two Hearts over One Heart.

Partner responds to the overcall according to the same principle as to a take-out double, bidding his best suit. In theory the overcall is game-forcing but players sometimes stop short when the bidding develops in an unfavourable way.

Defence against a One No-Trump opening

There are special dangers in overcalling an opponent's no-trump opening, for third hand, knowing his partner to have all-round strength, is well placed to double any intervention. Often he will double with trumps as moderate as K-x-x. To overcall in a suit, second hand should be strong in playing tricks.

(i) ♠ K Q J 9 6   (ii) ♠ J 7
     ♡ A 4   ♡ K J 9 7 6 4
     ◇ 7 5 2   ◇ K Q 6 4
     ♣ Q 6 3   ♣ 3

To overcall One No-Trump with Two Spades on (i) would be foolish at any score. There is no point in risking a penalty, for with the lead against a no-trump contract you have good prospects of defence. That cannot be said of hand (ii), for now your chances against Three No-Trumps are likely to depend on finding partner with an honour in hearts. Thus you may overcall with Two Hearts, at any rate if you are not vulnerable.

To double with a balanced hand is also dangerous, for here again you are in an exposed position. As a general rule, you should be at least 2 points stronger than the player whom you are doubling. Naturally you have to take into account whether his no-trump is weak or strong.

(iii) ♠ K J 4　　　　　　(iv) ♠ A 10 8 4
　　 ♡ A 10 7　　　　　　　　 ♡ 5
　　 ◇ K Q J 9 2　　　　　　　 ◇ K Q 10 7
　　 ♣ Q 6　　　　　　　　　　 ♣ A K 6 2

You could double a weak no-trump on (iii) because you have a fair suit to which you can retreat should partner respond in your weak suit, clubs.

You might double One No-Trump at Love All on (iv), but at any other score it would be wiser to pass. Partner is all too likely to rescue the double into Two Hearts and then you will have exchanged a good position for a bad one.

A double of One No-Trump is much closer to a penalty than to a take-out double. With a balanced hand partner should pass the double even if quite weak; he will not improve the situation by introducing a poor suit at the level of Two.

(v) ♠ Q 7 4 2　　　　　　(vi) ♠ K 6 4 3
　　♡ 10 5 3　　　　　　　　　♡ 5
　　◇ J 6 4　　　　　　　　　　◇ 9 7 3 2
　　♣ 5 3 2　　　　　　　　　　♣ 8 5 4 2

On (v) it is best to pass a double of One No-Trump. Partner may have the contract down in his own hand; in any event, it is unlikely that he will thank you for taking out the double into Two Spades.

Equally, on a stronger balanced hand, you should always pass, for it is a better proposition to defend against One No-Trump doubled than to try to make Three No-Trumps your way.

On (vi) you should take out the double into Two Clubs, giving your side the maximum space in which to find some sort of fit.

Overcalls in fourth position

So far in this chapter we have been considering overcalls by second hand after the right-hand opponent has opened. The situation of fourth player after an opening bid has been followed by two passes is quite different. He can bid much more freely, for there is an inference that partner has good values and in addition fourth hand is not so exposed to a penalty double.

In the examples that follow, assume the bidding to have gone:

South	West	North	East
1◇	Pass	Pass	?

Unless otherwise stated, the score is Love All.

(i)   ♠ K 4 2
     ♡ K J 10 6
     ◇ 5 3
     ♣ Q 10 7 4

(ii)   ♠ A K 6 3 2
     ♡ Q 4
     ◇ J 8
     ♣ A 10 4 2

On (i) the inexperienced player is apt to say to himself, 'They won't go far in One Diamond. I'm going to say "No bid" before they get together and bid a game in spades.'

That could happen – the game in spades – about once in twenty times, but meanwhile you would be missing several partscore and even game contracts your way. Remember that partner may have made a trap pass, diamonds being his best suit. You should therefore protect his pass by re-opening with One Heart or even with a shaded take-out double.

On (ii), if you were second in hand you would overcall with One Spade. In fourth hand you should double first to show that you are fairly strong and not just protecting. Quite often partner, with strength in diamonds, will be able to pass the double for penalties.

(iii)   ♠ K 7 5
     ♡ J 8 4
     ◇ K 9 6
     ♣ A 9 6 3

(iv)   ♠ 7 3
     ♡ K Q 10 7 6 4
     ◇ 4
     ♣ A J 7 3

Vulnerable, you would have to pass on (iii) for lack of a suitable call, but not vulnerable you can re-open with One No-Trump. The odds are that your side has the balance of the cards. The range for One No-Trump in the protective position is much lower than for a direct overcall.

On (iv) you should re-open with Two Hearts to show fair values.

Responding to partner's overcall

Partnership bidding in defence is, as it were, closer to the ground than in attack. Simple responses to partner's overcall are not forcing and should therefore indicate a playable contract. A jump in a new suit is generally treated as forcing for one round. The only game-forcing bid is a call of the enemy suit.

In the next two examples the bidding at Love All has gone:

South	West	North	East
1◇	1♡	2◇	?

(i)   ♠ K 10 6 4 2   (ii)   ♠ A 6 4
      ♡ 9 5 3   ♡ Q 10 2
      ◇ 6 2   ◇ J 9
      ♣ A J 8   ♣ A Q 7 6 3

On (i) simply raise to Two Hearts. It would be a mistake to introduce the moderate spades. Since overcalls are generally made on fairly good suits, less trump support is required than for opening bids.

On (ii) raise to Three Hearts. You should not dally with Three Clubs and risk being left on the wayside. That would show quite a different sort of hand – strong clubs and, by inference, little if any support for hearts; at least, that is the sensible interpretation, for in defence there is neither time nor space for bids that are just ornamental.

If partner had made an overcall at the two level, the bidding having gone 1♠ – 2♡ – Pass (or any other call), you would have a clear-cut raise to Four Hearts.

10

Competitive and Sacrifice Bidding

The use of take-out doubles in defence was described in the last chapter, but that is by no means the end of their story. They can be used by a player who has opened the bidding as well.

In general most doubles are for take-out, but now and then you will want to attempt to penalise your opponents by doubling them for penalties.

The double of an opening Three bid can have various shades of meaning according to the convention used. See 'Defences to Pre-emptive Bids' in Chapter 14.

These are some examples of the two kinds of double:

South	West	North	East
1♢	1♡	Pass	2♣
Double			

Although three suits have been mentioned, this is a take-out double. South has a strong hand with his main strength in diamonds and spades. North must respond accordingly.

South	West	North	East
1♡	Double	2♡	Pass
Pass	Double		

Here the same player doubles twice, each time for take-out.

South	West	North	East
1♡	Pass	1♠	Pass
2♡	Double		

The double of Two Hearts is for penalties, because West did not double hearts at the first opportunity.

South	West	North	East
1◇	Pass	2◇	Pass
Pass	Double		

Although West did not double One Diamond on the first round this double is for take-out. The auction has shown that both opponents are limited and West, knowing that his partner must have some strength, now decides to contest the partscore.

South	West	North	East
1♣	Pass	3♣	Double

This double at the level of Three is primarily a take-out double. East has had no chance to speak and is more likely to want to double for take-out than for penalties.

There are some sequences that cannot be classified one way or the other and can only be judged at the table. For example:

South	West	North	East
1♣	Pass	1NT	Pass
2♣	Double		

So far as theory goes, West might have a weak take-out double and have decided to contest after hearing the limited bidding of his opponents; or he might have a strong hand with good clubs and be doubling for penalties. East should be able to judge from his own cards and especially from his holding in clubs.

Action by third hand after a take-out double

One further aspect of take-out doubles is the auction by third hand after second hand has doubled. The bidding has gone:

South	West	North	East
1♡	Double	?	

North will now act as follows:

1 With a fair balanced hand, of around ten points North can redouble. Having the balance of power means we should be able to extract a fair penalty or play the hand.

(i)   ♠ K J 6   (ii)   ♠ A K 6 4
         ♡ 7 4   ♡ J
         ◇ A 10 7 2   ◇ Q 10 5 2
         ♣ Q 9 6 2   ♣ J 8 7 2

When he redoubles on (i) North will be looking towards the possibility of a penalty double. Suppose that East takes out into Two Clubs. South, if his hand is reasonably well suited to defence, should pass this round to North, who will double for penalties.

On (ii) North will be happy to double whichever suit the opponents choose to play in.

2 With a poor to moderate hand that includes support for partner's suit, North will raise to the limit.

(iii) ♠ 10 4   (iv) ♠ 4
     ♡ J 7 6 3   ♡ K 10 7 5
     ◇ Q 8 5 2   ◇ Q J 9 5 4
     ♣ 6 4 2   ♣ 7 3 2

On (iii), where without the intervention he would have passed, North can raise defensively to Two Hearts. On (iv) he can jump to Three Hearts; at favourable vulnerability – not vulnerable against vulnerable – he might even jump to Four.

3 As the raises to Two, Three and Four Hearts are preemptive in nature, the responder needs a way of showing a good raise in partner's suit. This can be done via a bid of 2NT, which is not needed in a natural sense as balanced hands of 10-12 points can start with a redouble.

(v) ♠ 7 2   (vi) ♠ 5
    ♡ K 8 5 4   ♡ Q J 10 3
    ◇ 9 5 3   ◇ K J 5 4
    ♣ A K J 7   ♣ A 10 9 4

Both these hands could start with 2NT. On (v) you would pass partner's reply of Three Hearts, but on (vi) you have enough to go on to game.

4 With a moderate to fair hand presenting a well-defined response, North will make his natural bid.

(vi) ♠ J 7 4   (vii) ♠ 10 4
     ♡ 10 6 3   ♡ 7 5
     ◇ K 10 5   ◇ A Q J 6 3
     ♣ A 6 4 2   ♣ Q 9 6 2

On (vi) North can make the normal response of 1NT. If the hand were slightly weaker he would pass.

On (vii) it is best to come in at once with Two Diamonds. Many players pass such hands but then only create difficulties for themselves. For example, East may bid One Spade and West Two Spades; now North has to guess whether or not to come in at the higher level.

These simple responses, are forcing for one round.

5   With a fair hand containing a good suit, North may jump in the suit, creating a game forcing situation.

(viii) ♠ A K Q 10 9 7 6   (ix) ♠ A K J 10 4
       ♡ 4   ♡ Q 4
       ◇ K 3 2   ◇ A Q 7 5 2
       ♣ J 5   ♣ 3

On (viii) a jump to Two Spades is best. This is forcing for one round.

Hand (ix) might start with a redouble, and Two Spades is also possible but a simple forcing bid of One Spade is probably best. Assuming partner rebids Two Hearts you can bid Three Diamonds, starting to give a fair picture of your hand.

Penalty doubles of low level contracts

Penalty doubles are deceiving in the sense that the safest and most profitable doubles are of low rather than of high contracts. It is seldom that you will catch a good player for 800 or 1100 at the level of Four or Five; and if you do, it will be a sacrifice bid and so the penalty will not be all profit. Even the best players will run into a big penalty every now and again at a low level, however; a player who declares that he never goes down more than 500 may be telling the truth but will be a losing player because he is not sufficiently aggressive.

The following are the elements that produce a good penalty of an intervening bid at a low level:

(a) Tricks in the trump suit.

(b) Shortage in partner's suit.

(c) Ability to cope with any subsequent double that partner may make.

The time honoured way of telling partner you were playing for a penalty was to double the intervening bid. However times change and a more subtle and better approach is available.

	South	West	North	East
	1♡	1♠	?	

(ix) ♠ 8 4 2
     ♡ J 5
     ◇ K J 5 3
     ♣ A 8 7

Without the intervention you would have bid 1NT, but you can hardly do that now with no spade stopper. You can't raise hearts on a doubleton and a forcing bid of Two Diamonds is more than you hand is worth. The solution is use a double by you at this point to show this type of hand, where the intervention has left you with no convenient bid. It is in effect a take out double by the responder, usually referred to as a negative double. (negative in the sense that you have no obvious support for partner.)

This begs the question of what to do when you have a full blooded penalty double of the opponents suit?

South	West	North	East
1♡	1♠	?	

(x) ♠ K Q 10 9 6
♡ 7 3
♢ Q 10 4
♣ A J 9

You would like to double Two Spades for penalties, but we have just said it is for take-out. The solution is to pass. Partner, who must be short in spades is expected to re-open with a double. If his hand is for example:

(xi) ♠ 5
♡ A K 8 4 2
♢ K 8 3 2
♣ Q 7 5

you will probably be taking tricks until Christmas.

Keep in mind that you need high cards as well as trumps to start playing for penalties at a low level.

South	West	North	East
1♡	2♢	?	

North holds:

(xii) ♠ 7
♡ 6 3
♢ K 10 9 7 4 2
♣ Q 8 4 3

(xiii) ♠ 6 4
♡ K 8 5
♢ K J 6 4 3
♣ Q 10 7

You cannot bid on (xii) and it is quite likely that partner will re-open with a double. It will probably then be best to bid Three Clubs, as if you pass the opponents may run to spades and partner may be tempted to double. Having no tricks outside diamonds it is better to pass for the present.

On hand (xiii) you would have had a reasonable pass of Two Diamonds had the opening been One Spade, waiting for partner to double, but when partner has bid hearts it is better to support him than wait. It may seem, on the surface, that by leading hearts you can establish a strong defence against a diamond contract; but declarer will simply accept the force and make all his trumps.

The concept of the negative double can be extended to cope with intervention at higher levels.

<table>
<tr><td>(xiv)♠ Q</td><td>(xv) ♠ A 10 6 2</td></tr>
<tr><td>♡ A 9 4 2</td><td>♡ A K 8 4 3</td></tr>
<tr><td>◇ K 10 6</td><td>◇ Q 7 4</td></tr>
<tr><td>♣ J 8 7 5 3</td><td>♣ 3</td></tr>
</table>

On (xiv), partner having opened One Spade, it is reasonable double an intervention of Two Diamonds. As you bid is for take out there is an inference that you have support for the unbid major. On (xv) partner opens One Club and the next player jumps to Two or even Three Diamonds. You may elect to double, making it clear you have good support for both majors.

Penalty doubles of high contracts

At higher levels the odds do not favour the doubler. Suppose, for example, that you double Four Spades and they just make it. The double has cost 170 points and if you had defeated them by one trick you would have gained only an extra 50; so, you are laying odds of nearly 7 to 2 on. If you light-heartedly double vulnerable opponents in Four Spades and they redouble and make an overtrick, that will cost you 810 points (930 instead of 150).

It follows that it is unwise to double high contracts unless you are fairly confident of defeating them. It is particularly unwise to double high suit contracts on the strength of high cards held by you in the side suits. When you have a couple of ace-kings and a king, and opponents contract voluntarily for Four Hearts, respect their intelligence to the point of assuming that they have exceptional distribution. They do, after all, know that these aces and kings are not in their own hands.

In that last sentence lies the crux of the matter. It is when, from the pattern of your own hand, you can tell that the declarer will run into [i]unexpected trouble that there may be a good case for a speculative double. The standard example is when opponents bid, say, Four Hearts, and you have Q-J-10-9 of hearts. That affords much better basis for a double than would three side aces.

By the same token, it is a beginner's mistake to double a slam contract because he has an ace and a king-queen, or two aces. In these days the one thing that even the weakest players bring to market is some sort of ace-showing convention and if they neglect to use it the assumption is that they have a void suit. Moreover, if you double Six Hearts and defeat it by one trick you gain an extra 50; if they redouble and make it you lose an extra 590. Since doubling for penalties is such an unprofitable venture, a double of a slam, as we shall see in Chapter 14, is often invested with a conventional meaning.

Redoubling for rescue

Just as a double is sometimes for penalties, sometimes for take-out, so a redouble can be used as a sign of distress as well as an expression of confidence. The so-called 'SOS redouble' occurs at a low level when it is apparent that if the double suited him the player would pass. These are some typical sequences:

South	West	North	East
1♣	Double	Pass	Pass
Redouble			

West has doubled One Club for take-out and East has made it a penalty pass, showing very strong clubs. South, having opened a short club suit, asks partner to rescue.

South	West	North	East
1♡	1♠	Double	1NT
Double	Pass	Pass	Redouble

The inference to be drawn from this auction is that East is not keen to play in One No-Trump doubled. He redoubles in the hope of finding a safer harbour in one of the minor suits.

It will be noted that in both these sequences the doubled contract has been passed by partner before the redouble. That is a usual condition for a rescue redouble. The following sequence has a different meaning:

South	West	North	East
1♡	Pass	Pass	Double
Redouble			

Here South has not, so far, been doubled for penalties at all, so his redouble is a natural call, signifying a strong hand.

Redoubling for business

So far as mathematics go, the odds favour a player who contemplates a redouble in a close situation. If you redouble Four Spades and make it you gain an extra 290; if you are one down not vulnerable, it costs you an extra 100. Vulnerable, the odds are not so good: 240 to 200.

It follows from this that when opponents have not entered the auction and there is no likelihood of their finding a sacrifice at a high level, then it is right to redouble if you are unlikely to go more than one down.

More often, however, contracts are doubled after a competitive auction. Then it becomes unwise to redouble, however confident you may be, for if the enemy take out the redouble it is unlikely that you will exact a penalty anything like so rewarding as if you had been left in to make your doubled game.

It is therefore exactly true, and not just an engaging paradox, that after a competitive auction a good time to redouble is when you expect to go [i]one down in your own contract but are sure that you can take good care of any further venture by the opposition.

Sacrifice bidding

In competitive situations so much depends on judgement, experience and what the French call *présence à la table* (by which they really mean alertness to every mannerism and intonation), that one can write only in general terms. First, it is important to know the true value of game in various vulnerability situations.

When all factors have been taken into consideration, an approximate estimation of the value of a game, including the trick score and the equity value, is as follows:

(a) At Love All, about 420.

(b) The equalising game when one side is game up, self-evidently the same 420.

(c) The second game to a side that is already game up, about 500 – not the 820 or so that will be entered on the score-sheet.

(d) The rubber game at Game All, precisely the 620 or so that is entered on the score-sheet.

From these figures it follows that it pays to go down 300 to save the game at any stage and 500 to save the rubber game.

Regarding the matter from the other side, there is profit in accepting a 500 penalty at Love All or when game down; when game up, you break about even; at Game All, you show a slight loss.

In a competitive situation, when the choice is between, say, doubling opponents in Four Spades or going on to Five Hearts or passing, these are sound principles to follow:

(a) If confident you can defeat them, double rather than try for a doubtful game. Better a safe 300 than a problematical 450 or so, which may be minus 100 instead.

(b) When you are reasonably sure that they will make their contract, bid on even though the sacrifice may be expensive. It is not a tragedy if you lose 700 to save a game and there is a chance that the opponents will make a mistake, either failing to double or not defending well or even bidding one higher. Keep them at full stretch.

(c) When fairly confident that you can make your contract, bid it rather than accept a penalty. The opponents may add to your score by doubling or they may go one higher.

(d) In doubtful situations, when you are not sure who can make what, always press on. If you are wrong, in that you are one down and they would have been one down, the cost is small. If they would have made their game and you are one down, you have gained appreciably. If they would have made their game and you make yours, you have gained enormously. There is the further point that when both contracts are 'off' the enemy may misjudge the situation and make a phantom sacrifice — that is, a sacrifice against a contract that would have gone down.

At the slam level there is a theoretical profit in sacrificing to the extent of 900 to save a non-vulnerable small slam and up to about 1300 to save a vulnerable slam; but since one is seldom entirely sure that the opponents will make their slam it is generally unwise at rubber bridge to invite such a penalty for a small comparative gain.

11
Partscore Situations

Partscores appear deceptively small on the score-sheet; 40 points here, 60 points there; yet the way they are handled will have a decisive effect on a player's fortunes in rubber bridge and they represent the area in which a good player's advantage is greatest. In this chapter we shall be concerned not just with how to bid when one side has a partscore but with how to fight for a partscore and how to assess its value.

Value of a partscore

Any partscore has, of course, a hidden value beyond the points recorded for it. Up to 30 the hidden value is inconsiderable – not more than 40 points or so. From 40 onwards (there is not much practical difference between 40 and a higher score) the hidden value rises from about 70 at Love All up to (some say) 200 at Game All, where the prize of the eventual game is higher and the opposition, being vulnerable, will not be so free to compete. Since the trick score has to be added, it follows that the real difference, at Game All, between your side registering 60 and the enemy registering 60 is in the region of 260 plus 260 – i.e. over 500.

When one side only has a partscore, that has a considerable bearing on sacrifice bidding at the game level. A side that has a partscore of 60 should be more ready to accept a penalty and preserve its partscore advantage for the next hand. For some reason, most players do the opposite. 'I thought we'd take the game,' they tell you smugly after taking you out of a double that would have brought in 500 and left you in possession of your partscore.

In the same way, when opponents have the partscore and so are already halfway towards game, one should not risk a big penalty to prevent them from converting the partscore. Here again, most players construe the matter in an opposite sense: an enemy partscore provokes them to an unusual degree of combativeness.

Fighting for a partscore

Did you note, I wonder, the following sentence in Chapter 9, relating to a hand on which an immediate overcall was not advised? 'You may have the opportunity to enter the bidding later after opponents have shown that they are limited in strength.'

Therein lies the essence of competitive bidding at the partscore level. The bidding goes:

South	West	North	East
1♡	Pass	2♡	Pass
Pass	?		

West holds:

(i) ♠ K 7 4
    ♡ 6 3
    ◇ A 10 5 2
    ♣ K J 6 3

(ii) ♠ 7 4
    ♡ 5 2
    ◇ A Q 10 7 3
    ♣ K J 9 6

since the opponents have dropped the bidding in Two Hearts West can deduce that his partner has some strength. On (i) he should re-open with a take-out double.

On (ii) the best bid, actually, is 2NT. This cannot be a natural call on values, for West has passed One Heart; since it bypasses Two Spades, the inference that partner should draw is that West proposes to contest in one of the minor suits.

More risky, but still to be recommended, is this sort of intervention when 'under the gun' – that is, when the opponents have not stopped bidding.

South	West	North	East
1◇	Pass	1♠	Pass
2♣	Pass	2◇	?

East holds:

    ♠ A J 6 4
    ♡ K Q 8 5 3
    ◇ 6 2
    ♣ Q 4

East should reckon that if he passes at this point the opponents will probably gain the contract in Two Diamonds, since partner is hardly likely to be sufficiently strong to compete on his own. Having bid the other two suits South is unlikely to have good hearts, so a bid of Two Hearts now is at any rate less risky than it would have been on the preceding round.

It should be added that the kind of aggressive bids described in this section are not part of the repertoire of average players. That, if one is to be sententious, is why they are only average players.

Opening bids in partscore situations

The general principle to follow is the same in all partscore situations: be aggressive – not so much because there is less far to go for game as because it is both safer and more effective to speak early than late.

Of weak hands – borderline openings – it can be said at once that whatever the score both sides should strive to be into the bidding early.

As dealer, at 40 up, you hold:

(iii)	♠ K J 6 3	(iv)	♠ 10 5
	♡ 7 2		♡ A J 7 3
	◇ A 10 4		◇ K 10 6 2
	♣ K J 9 5		♣ A 6 3

On hand (iii) not only should you open but you should choose the aggressive bid, One Spade. With no partscore that would be unsound, but at 40 up you are not obliged to rebid if partner goes Two Hearts. The advantage of opening One Spade is twofold: you may snatch game in Two Spades, and by bidding this suit you make it more difficult for second hand to overcall than had you opened One Club. For the same sort of reason, on (iv), you can open 1NT. That is always the most difficult bid for an opponent to counter.

When the enemy have the partscore an opening bid is still the best defence. Not only that, but it is safer to open a moderate hand than to attempt a brave defence at the three level when the opponents have made the first two bids.

As to stronger hands, an opening of Two Clubs at 60 up has the same sense as with no partscore. Other Two bids are strong in principle but the range may be extended for tactical reasons.

Constructive bidding from a partscore

Constructive bidding from a partscore, especially a low score like 30 or 40, has its pitfalls: the way to avoid them is to use, for the most part, the same language of bidding as when there is no partscore.

In the following examples your side has a partscore and your partner has opened One Heart.

(v) ♠ 10 8 7 4   (vi) ♠ K 10 8
     ♡ J 9 6 2   ♡ J 7 3
     ◇ A 7 4   ◇ A Q 4
     ♣ 10 3   ♣ K J 10 6

On hand (v) raise to Two Hearts not only at 60 up but also at 80 up. If the worst apparently happens – you are overboard by one trick – you can be sure that you would not have bought the contract had you passed One Heart.

On (vi) there can be a slam if partner is strong. The best foundation for any future bidding, whether you are 40 up or 60 up, is to give a picture of your hand by responding 2NT.

(vii) ♠ A 6   (viii) ♠ Q 6
      ♡ K 10 8 4   ♡ A 9 7
      ◇ Q J 7 3   ◇ K J 6 4
      ♣ K 6 2   ♣ A K 8 5

On (vii) respond Three Hearts even when this carries you over score. The opener will take this as encouraging but not forcing.

On (viii) make your normal force of Three Clubs. This jump in a new suit has its usual meaning. There is no such thing as 'bidding to the score'. If partner simply repeats his hearts you can give him further encouragement by raising to Four Hearts.

12

Bidding to Game and Slam

The first problem, in slam bidding, is to judge when a slam may be possible in some denominations. These are a few tests that can be applied on different occasions:

The point-count test

On the 4-3-2-1 count there are 40 points in the pack and a side that has 34 will usually have a good play for Six No-Trumps even without the help of a long suit.

Suppose, therefore, that your partner opens One No-Trump and you have a 17-count 4-3-3-3 hand. Since the most you can have between you is 31 you don't have to think about a slam. But if you have 21 points, then you would know that you had a minimum of 33 and would press strongly for a slam.

Combinations that provide a slam

Not many hands, however, yield to the sort of reckoning described above. Most slams result from an ever-varying combination of playing tricks and controls.

You may recall that we found in Chapter 7 that an opening bid opposite an opening bid would usually produce a game. It is not a method that experienced players use, but a similar test can be applied to slams. The rule now is that an opening bid on one side, plus the values for a jump rebid on the other, should put the partnership in the slam zone. So, let us say that you respond One Spade to One Heart and partner jumps to Three Hearts: if you have close to an opening bid and the hands are not a palpable misfit you must try for a slam.

By using a sort of leeway principle, you can apply this test to many combinations in which the strength is differently distributed. For example, partner opens with a Two bid and you have two aces but less than an opening bid. Partner should have rather more than for a jump rebid, so again the two hands will contain between them the values for a jump rebid plus an opening bid. Variations of this test will occur in the examples below.

Cue-bids and Blackwood

In the chapters on defensive overcalls and competitive bidding we found that a defender would sometimes bid his opponent's suit to show first-round control – either ace or void. That sort of control-showing bid, not necessarily in a suit called by the opponents, is very common in slam bidding. Once a trump suit has been agreed, as by a raise from One to Three, the bid of a new suit, often called a 'cue-bid', may show not a genuine suit but just a control.

There are also ways of showing a number of controls by means of a single bid. The popular Blackwood convention, which we shall have to describe in advance of Part IV, is an example. In this convention a bid of Four No-Trumps is in most circumstances a request to partner to show how many aces he holds. With no aces (also with four aces) partner will respond Five Clubs, with one ace Five Diamonds, with two aces Five Hearts, and three Aces Five Spades. After a bid of Five No-Trumps the same performance takes place in respect of kings.

If you noticed a slight edge to the use of the word 'performance' in the last sentence, that is because the Blackwood convention is much over used. When one has solid suits and the only doubt concerns the top controls, then it is sensible enough to use an ace-demanding convention. But more often, at the slam level, one is worried not just about aces but about the strength of the trump suit, a missing king or queen in a side suit, an extra ruffing trick, and so on; to reach the right answer on hands of that sort (and they are the vast majority) it is essential to exchange information by way of natural and not conventional bids.

In the following examples West is the dealer and the score is Love All.

(i)   An immediate cue-bid in the opponents' suit

♠ A Q 8 7 4   ♠ K 10 3 2
♡ A J   ♡ K 9 7 4 2
◇ 7 4 2   ◇ –
♣ J 10 2   ♣ A Q 9 3

The bidding goes:

South	West	North	East
–	1♠	2◇	3◇(1)
Pass	3♠	Pass	4♣(2)
Pass	4♡(3)	Pass	5◇(4)
Pass	5♠	Pass	6♠
All Pass			

(1) East has an ideal hand for a forcing cue-bid in the opponent's suit. The bid initially suggests good support for spades. This cue-bid should not be overdone: with an alternative suit and only fair support for partner it is better to make a normal force in the other suit.

(2) This confirms that spades are going to be trumps and denotes a control rather than a biddable suit.

(3) Although West has a minimum opening he can well afford to show his heart ace below the game level.

(4) Again a control-showing bid. From East's point of view if partner has the king of clubs there may be a grand slam.

Note that the two hands contain only 24 points between them. The slam would be difficult to reach without the intervention by North. Six Spades is not a certainty but it would be unlucky to fail.

(ii)   A cue-bid to confirm responder's suit

♠ 3   ♠ K 7 4
♡ A Q J 4 3   ♡ 6 2
◇ A Q 6   ◇ 10 7 6
♣ K 10 9 7   ♣ A Q J 5 2

The bidding goes:

South	West	North	East
–	1♡	1♠	2♣
Pass	2♠(1)	Pass	2NT
Pass	3♣	Pass	4♣(2)
Pass	5♣(3)	All Pass	

(1) This is the economical way to show support for clubs and a game-going hand. First-round control of the opponent's suit is not guaranteed in this position. The bid is primarily a means of forcing to game.

(2) East can scarcely repeat no-trumps with nothing in diamonds and only one stop in spades, so he makes a minimum bid in clubs.

(3) West can be sure that he is missing one or both of the red kings and an ace, so he is content to stop in Five Clubs.

In general, it is a fair proposition to bid a slam on an even chance. Not vulnerable, the slam bonus is 500 and the loss if the slam fails is about 450 for the game missed plus a penalty of 50. However, it is wise to keep on the right side of these odds, so far as one can judge, for many slams that are described as being 'on a finesse' are in fact worse than even chances: there is usually some other hazard, such as an unexpected ruff or a 5-0 break in the trump suit. Six Clubs on the last hand, for example, does not depend just on the heart finesse: the hearts must break evenly as well for twelve tricks to be comfortable.

(iii) A hand for Blackwood

♠ K J 10 7 4   ♠ A 9
♡ K Q 3   ♡ 7
◇ K 7 6 2   ◇ A Q 10 8 4 3
♣ Q   ♣ K J 6 2

The bidding goes:

West	East
1♠	2◇
3◇	4NT(1)
5♣	5◇
Pass	

(1) The diamond support greatly strengthens East's hand. He has good hopes of a slam now, for partner is likely to have an ace and the king of diamonds, or two aces, or some other values that will make the slam on a finesse at worst. However, as a precaution, East puts in a Blackwood Four No-Trumps and discovers that, contrary to expectation, partner has no ace at all.

(iv) A borderline grand slam

♠ A 8 4
♡ A 10
◇ K 9 6 2
♣ K Q 7 4

♠ K Q 7 6 5
♡ K 7 3
◇ A 8 4
♣ A 10

The bidding goes:

West	East
1♣	2♠
3♠(1)	4♣
4♡	5◇
6◇	7♠(2)
Pass	

(1) When partner forces in spades West can at once visualise a likely slam. He does not have to think long about his next bid – Three Spades is clearly best – but as an experiment let us observe how the two tests mentioned at the beginning of the chapter could be applied at this point. West has 16 points and his partner is likely to have as much for his force. That makes an expectancy of 32 points and in addition West has strong controls, support for his partner's suit, and a ruffing trick. Also, do the hands meet the test of 'opening bids plus jump rebid'? Surely, for West can spare a king and still have an opening bid, and if a king were added to partner's force the general values would be fully equal to a jump rebid.

(2) After this exchange of cue-bids East can place his partner with two aces, king of diamonds (or possibly a singleton), and no doubt king of clubs, for without that card West would not be bidding so freely. As West will have a club suit of some kind, there should be ways of taking care of the red-suit losers. Thus it seems that the grand slam will depend at worst on finding a reasonable break in spades, assuming partner to have A-x-x.

The contract will, in fact, depend on the spades being 3-2. That is 68% chance, just better than 2 to 1 on, and the grand slam is a reasonable venture since those odds accord precisely with the odds that a player needs to have in his favour. At Game All, for example, a successful grand slam will bring in an extra 750; if it fails, the indirect loss is 1530.

The effect of this is that grand slams should be bid only when a player can practically count thirteen tricks. On the present hand most pairs would be content, rightly enough, to play in Six.

(v) Stopping in Five

♠ A K J 8 4 3   ♠ Q 10 7
♡ A K J 9 2   ♡ 8 4
◇ —   ◇ A K 7 4 3
♣ Q 5   ♣ 10 6 3

The bidding goes:

West	East
2♠	3◇
3♡	4♠(1)
5♠(2)	Pass(3)

(1) Three Spades would be forcing in this sequence, but East is right to take the opportunity to show that he has positive support for spades.

(2) The two losers in the unbid suit obviously represent the danger to a slam, and a bid of Five in the established trump suit is the way to convey that message. Note that it would be pointless to use Blackwood here, for if partner's response were to show one ace West would not know which ace and also would not know about second-round control of clubs.

(3) From his partner's failure to bid Four No-Trumps East draws the correct inference that his ace of diamonds is duplicated by a void. If West had had two singletons in the minors, no doubt he would have asked about aces.

If, instead of the ace-king of diamonds, East had had the king-jack of diamonds and the king of clubs, he would have realised that the king of clubs was the critical card and would have bid Six.

(vi)   Two Clubs followed by 3NT

♠ A K   ♠ J 7 4
♡ A J 8   ♡ Q 6 5
◇ A K Q 10 4   ◇ 8 3 2
♣ K Q 7   ♣ A 10 6 4

The bidding goes:

West	East
2♣	2◇(1)
3NT	4NT(2)
5◇(3)	5NT(4)
6NT	Pass

(1) Though he has a few scattered points East is not quite worth a positive response of 2NT.

(2) Partner's rebid of Three No-Trumps after a Two Club opening suggests upwards of 25 points. With 7 points East must give his partner another chance. This is one of the situations in which Four No-Trumps is obviously not Blackwood.

(3) With a strong suit in addition to his 26 points, West naturally accepts the slam suggestion.

(4) This bid is on the cautious side: with a reliable partner who would not forget the original negative Two Diamonds, East could show his ace of clubs now.

(vii) A forcing pass

```
♠ A K Q 10 6 2        ♠ 7
♡ Q 10                ♡ A K J 9 7 6 3
◇ 4                   ◇ 6 2
♣ A J 10 5            ♣ Q 7 4
```

The bidding goes:

South	West	North	East
–	2♠	5◇	5♡
6◇	Pass(1)	Pass	6♡(2)
Pass	Pass	7◇(3)	Double
All Pass			

West adopts a manoeuvre that is common at all stages of competitive bidding – the forcing pass. It is clear that East/West have the balance of the cards and that North/South are sacrificing. By passing Six Diamonds West says to his partner: 'I have some support for you and quite possibly we can make Six Hearts. I leave it to you whether to bid Six Hearts or double.'

(2) East knows that his partner would not be making a forcing pass if in addition to missing the ace-king of hearts he had two losers in diamonds. So, as his hearts are good, East bids the slam. There is a further psychological reason for bidding Six: opponents who bid Six Diamonds over Five Hearts will almost always, as an insurance against a heavy loss, go to Seven Diamonds over Six Hearts.

(3) And so it turns out.

Part III
Bidding Systems and
Conventions

13
Bidding Systems

The bidding methods set out in Part II represent, it will be understood, only one way of playing the game. The conventional Two Club opening and the general style of bidding belong to what is known somewhat vaguely as the 'Two Club' system. This is the most commonly played method in Britain and for the rest of this chapter is referred to as 'British style'.

Other systems cannot be described, naturally, in a few pages and one must refer the reader to various learned tomes. All that is intended in this chapter is to give sufficient account of the most widely played systems to enable a player to understand what opponents are doing and even to adapt his own game.

Acol system

By far the most widely played system in the British tournament world is that known as 'Acol'. The groundwork of bidding as presented in this book is that of the Acol system, though there are, of course, various additional refinements practised by tournament players.

The Acol use of Two bids is slightly different, however. The Two Club opening is as described in Chapter 8, but other Two bids are forcing for one round. The weakness response is 2NT. The Acol Two bid denotes what the book calls 'a hand of power and quality'.

Strong Club Systems

Since the earliest days of contract there have been systems in which One Club is used as a conventional opening on strong hands. The One Club opening promises upwards of 16 points or so. The weakness response, on less than 8 points, is one Diamond. Any positive response is game-forcing. In some One Club systems Two Diamonds is also a conventional bid, forcing to game. An opening of Two Clubs shows a club suit; Two Hearts and Two Spades show a good suit but insufficient high cards for a One Club opening.

In the tournament world the most popular of these systems are Precision Club and Blue Team Club, but there are innumerable variations.

Five Card Majors

There are many variations within the framework of a five card major system and overall they are the most widely used methods in the world. An opening bid of 1♡/1♠ requires at least five cards in the suit and an opening bid of One No-Trump is generally in the range of 15–17 or 16–18 points. If the hand does not contain a five card major or the values for One No-Trump then the opening bid has to be in a minor suit of at least three cards.

One Club Systems

There are many systems which use an opening bid of One Club as a preparatory move on a variety of hands. Almost all of them include a weak balanced hand in the range of 12–15/16 points in the opening bid. The most popular today is the Polish Club.

14

Special Conventions

The account of bidding in Part II included very few artificial conventions. The opening bid of Two Clubs is artificial, and so is the Two Diamond response. The Blackwood convention described in the chapter on slam bidding is artificial, and so, though it is so familiar that one is apt to overlook the fact, is the take-out double. Manoeuvres such as cue-bids and game-forcing overcalls do not come into quite the same category.

Let it be said at once that the game can be played very capably with no more conventions than those just mentioned. However, there are many others that are widely played and useful to varying degrees. They can be grouped under the following headings: defence to pre-emptive bids; slam conventions; artificial responses to 1NT; lead-directing doubles.

Defence to pre-emptive bids

A pre-emptive bid is awkward in the sense that it takes away much of the room generally required to develop the auction in a constructive way. The most reliable way of coping with these high level openings is to use a double for takeout. This allows all the other bids to remain as natural, even 3NT.

Let us suppose that in all the following examples South opens Three Clubs and West holds:

<blockquote>

(i)   ♠ K J 7 4　　　　　(ii)   ♠ A 10 4
      ♡ A 8 5 2　　　　　　　　 ♡ K 7
      ◇ A K 10 6　　　　　　　　 ◇ A K Q 10 5
      ♣ 5　　　　　　　　　　　 ♣ A 7 4

</blockquote>

On (i) it is clear that a take-out double is the perfect way to describe the West hand. If East has a useful hand with nine or more points he should be in a position to bid game, or with good clubs to convert the double and play for penalties by passing.

With (ii) West should bid a direct 3NT. You are hoping partner will provide enough bits and pieces to see you arrive at nine tricks. It would be quite wrong to bid Three Diamonds, as partner, holding no more say than the ace of hearts and the jack of diamonds would have no reason to bid.

(iii)	♠ K Q 5	(iv)	♠ A J 10 8 6 3
	♡ A K 10 9 8 7 4		♡ K 10 9
	◇ A J 10		◇ A 4
	♣ 8		♣ 7 2

Hand (iii) is too good for a simple overcall. West should bid a direct Four Hearts, taking the strain off East. The principle is as in the previous example, of not leaving partner to guess what to do with a few scattered values. On (iv) West overcalls Three Spades. This may turn out badly if North has the balance of power, but it is a risk you have to take when confronted by a pre-emptive opening.

If you are strong in the opponent's suit but without the values to bid Three No-Trumps then you must pass, hoping that partner may be able to re-open when you will happily pass for penalties. As a corollary, partner should be prepared to pass your initial double holding scattered values and some length in the enemy suit.

(v)	♠ K 7 3	(vi)	♠ 8 4 2
	♡ A 10 5		♡ K 9 5
	◇ A 7 4		◇ Q 6 3
	♣ K J 10 5		♣ A 10 8 4

Looking at (v) it is clear you must pass an opening bid of Three Clubs hoping partner will double. With (vi) if West doubles an opening bid of Three Clubs it would be correct for East to pass, expecting to collect a fair penalty.

Slam conventions

We have already described the Blackwood Four No-Trump convention. It has been modified in recent times to reflect the importance that is attached to the possession of the trump honours and the variation that is currently in favour rejoices in the name of Roman Key Card Blackwood.

In this method the king of the agreed trump suit is counted as an ace or key card and possession of the queen of trumps can also be shown or denied. The responses after Four No-Trumps are:

5♣	0 or 3 key cards
5◇	1 or 4 key cards
5♡	2 or 5 key cards but no queen of trumps
5♠	2 or 5 key cards and the queen of trumps

The reader will be ahead of me here in realising that the key cards are the four aces and the king of the agreed trump suit.

As the responses of Five Clubs and Five Diamonds say nothing about the queen of trumps it is possible for the enquirer to ascertain if it is held by making the cheapest bid which is not a sign off. For example:

West	East
2♠	3♠
4NT	5◇
5♡	

In this sequence Five Hearts asks East about the queen of spades. The first step, Five Spades, denies it, the second, Five No-Trumps would show it.

Artificial responses to 1NT

As was foreshadowed in the discussion of no-trump openings in Chapter 6, there are conventional ways of discovering a fit after an opening bid of 1NT. The best-known method is the Stayman convention, in which Two Clubs is an artificial response asking the opener to show a four-card major. If he has none, the opener rebids Two Diamonds. In some variations the opener can rebid Two No-Trumps to show a maximum no-trump with a strong minor suit.

Many players use Three Clubs over Two No-Trumps in a similar sense. When the opener's only four-card suit is clubs he rebids Three No-Trumps.

Transfers

Whilst the rubber bridge players' text is 'Stayman and Blackwood', that of his tournament playing counterpart is undoubtedly 'Stayman and Transfers'.

It was Oswald (Ozzie) Jacoby who was responsible for the introduction into the game of one of the cornerstones of modern bidding, the Jacoby Transfer.

He recognised that a natural response to an opening bid of One No-Trump meant that the opening lead would be through the strong hand. How much better it would be if the hand could be played from the other side. His solution, the Jacoby Transfer proved to have a far-reaching effect on the way hands have been bid ever since.

The idea is as follows:

After an opening bid of One No-Trump responder bids either Two Diamonds, asking the opener to bid Two Hearts, or Two Hearts requesting the opener to reply Two Spades. In both cases the responder will have a five card or longer suit in the major opener has been asked to bid.

The advantage of this method is that it allows the No-Trump bidder to play the hand, thereby protecting his high cards from the opening lead. Less obviously it gives you room to investigate the best game contract and it also permits you to explore for a possible slam, usually without getting past the all-important 3NT.

The only concession you make is the loss of a natural bid of Two Diamonds, a small price to pay.

Remember that because you are forcing your partner to respond in a particular way you have no information about the quality of the support that you will find for your suit. The only certainty you have is that partner having opened 1NT, your five-card suit will be sure to be facing a doubleton.

Transfers offer a significant advantage over standard methods as many additional sequences are available:

West	East
1NT	2♢
2♡	

Now East can choose between:

Pass	Weak with hearts
2♠	Four spades, five hearts, forcing for one round
2NT	Invitational raise with five hearts
3♣	Four Clubs, five hearts, forcing
3♢	Four Diamonds, five hearts, forcing
3NT	Natural with five hearts
4♡	Natural, at least six hearts.

It is equally possible to play Transfers after an opening bid of 2NT, the responder using Three Diamonds and Three Hearts.

Lead-directing doubles

As was noted in the discussion of penalty doubles in Chapter 10, a double of a slam contract is mathematically a poor proposition for the doubler. In consequence, a double of a slam, when not an obvious sacrifice, is used to attract a particular lead. This convention, known as the Lightner slam double, is universally used by good players.

The Lightner double asks partner to find a surprise lead: not a trump, not a suit bid by the defending side, nor (when that would be the obvious lead) an unbid suit. Sometimes the double is based on a void, sometimes on tricks held in a side suit bid by the opponents. In particular, partner's attention is directed towards the possibility of leading the first suit bid by the dummy.

The Lightner double does not apply at the game level, but there too a double of Three No-Trumps – sometimes also of Two No-Trumps – may have lead-directing significance. This is especially so when there is a surprise element in the double, as in the following sequence:

South	West	North	East
Pass	1♡	Pass	1♠
Pass	2NT	Pass	3NT
Double	All Pass		

Here South has doubled Three No-Trumps although he passed originally and he partner has not made a bid. Obviously, he is telling his partner that the only hope for the defence lies in a spade lead.

After a competitive auction doubles of Three No-Trumps do not, like the Lightner double, ask for a surprise lead. When the doubler has bid a suit, the double emphasises that that suit should be led. When only the opening leader has bid, the double again proposes that that suit should be led.

Part IV
Tactical Moves in Play

15

Guessing and Finessing

'These experts are so lucky – they always seem to guess right,' said the old lady attending her first bridge tournament. And what she said was true. No-one can make a king sit on the right side of a queen, but when there is a choice of plays a good player will almost always find some indications, however slight. In practice, a complete guess is very rare. When there is no discernible clue it is sometimes possible to create one. Take this simple example of a two-way finesse:

```
              A 10 8 4
   Q 5 3                7 6
              K J 9 2
```

As we saw in an earlier chapter, the odds favour a finesse for the queen rather than a play for the drop. South can finesse in either direction and he can improve his chances slightly by playing off a top card in case there be a singleton queen.

The best practical line is to play on West's nerves by leading the jack from hand. If the cards lay differently, South having J-x or J-x-x, it would be right for West to cover. So, he may solve declarer's worry by putting the queen on the jack. If he is not a strong player he may hesitate for a moment before playing low. It is not unfair to take advantage of that sort of hesitation.

Digressing for a moment – for this is an important matter – it would not be right for a defender who had two or three small cards to hesitate deliberately in order to mislead the declarer. At the same time, against a good opponent that sort of hesitation is a blunder as well as a crime. It may deceive him the first time, but never again. A good bridge player has to acquire a poker player's faculty of observation.

Returning to the diagram, the principle that emerges is that when declarer wants to tempt a cover he should lead a high card. Clearly, in the present example, the lead of the nine by South would put no strain on West. This is another common situation:

```
                A 3 2
    K 7 5                      10 8 6 4
                Q J 9
```

Since he would welcome a cover that would give him a chance to finesse the nine on the way back, South should lead the queen rather than the jack. It is true that West will normally not cover, for he would not expect South to lead an unsupported queen; but every now and again, at a suit contract, the only hope will be to slip through the queen from Q-x, so there is always some pressure on West when the queen is led.

The corollary is that when declarer wants to avoid a cover he should lead the lowest card of his sequence.

```
                A K 7 6 2
    Q 5 3                      9 8 4
                J 10
```

Playing no-trumps, with no side entry to the table, South's best chance of making five tricks is to slip through the ten – not the jack, which is more likely to be covered. Once the queen has been played the best that South can do, with no entry to dummy, is to duck and hope to make four tricks that way.

When there is more than one way to play a suit and declarer has to determine who has the critical card, an opponent's silence in the bidding is often one of the most eloquent signs.

Game All; Dealer West

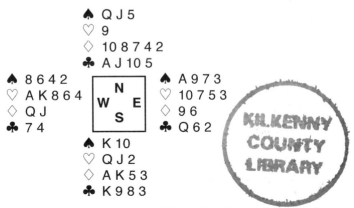

```
                    ♠ Q J 5
                    ♡ 9
                    ◇ 10 8 7 4 2
                    ♣ A J 10 5
    ♠ 8 6 4 2                      ♠ A 9 7 3
    ♡ A K 8 6 4         N          ♡ 10 7 5 3
    ◇ Q J           W     E        ◇ 9 6
    ♣ 7 4               S          ♣ Q 6 2
                    ♠ K 10
                    ♡ Q J 2
                    ◇ A K 5 3
                    ♣ K 9 8 3
```

West deals and passes, and so do North and East. South might open One No-Trump on his 16 points, but One Diamond is at least as good. West has too many losers for a vulnerable overcall and should pass. North raises to Three Diamonds. Now South will probably try for Three No-Trumps, though not with great confidence.

West opens his normal fourth best, the six of hearts. Dummy plays the nine, East the ten, and South the queen.

South must find his nine tricks quickly. It is no use playing on spades, for then the opponents will surely take at least four hearts and the ace of spades.

Declarer's luck holds when the diamonds break 2-2. Now the contract depends on finding the queen of clubs.

South will play off his diamond winners and then review the evidence. The play to the first trick has marked West with the ace-king of hearts, for if East had had either of those cards he would have played it. West has also turned up with the queen-jack of diamonds.

That is already sufficient reason for South to play East for the queen of clubs. West, although probably holding a fair heart suit and the two honours in diamonds, has neither opened the bidding nor overcalled at the one level. With the queen of clubs in addition, he might have done so. Apart from this negative inference from the bidding, there is a general probability in favour of the high cards being divided.

Inference from length

On the last hand declarer obtained his clue by estimating the strength of the defending hands. Equally common are indications based on length.

Love All; Dealer South

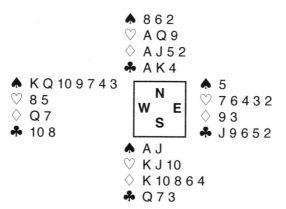

```
              ♠ 8 6 2
              ♡ A Q 9
              ◇ A J 5 2
              ♣ A K 4
♠ K Q 10 9 7 4 3        ♠ 5
♡ 8 5            N      ♡ 7 6 4 3 2
◇ Q 7        W     E    ◇ 9 3
♣ 10 8          S      ♣ J 9 6 5 2
              ♠ A J
              ♡ K J 10
              ◇ K 10 8 6 4
              ♣ Q 7 3
```

South opens One No-Trump and West overcalls with Two Spades. North has 18 points; added to his partner's 13–15, that makes an expectancy of about 32. North would not be wrong to settle for Three No-Trump, but the chances for a slam are, if anything, improved by West's intervention, which will help South to place the cards. North might bid Four No-Trump

– a natural raise, not Blackwood; the fact that he has no guard in spades scarcely matters, for North is so strong in the other suits that he can be almost sure his partner has ace or king of spades.

An alternative that leaves the decision open is Three Spades, an overcall in the enemy suit. If partner bids Three No-Trumps North can raise to Four No-Trumps and South goes on to Six No-Trumps. So the full bidding is:

South	West	North	East
1NT	2♠	3♠	Pass
3NT	Pass	4NT	Pass
6NT	All Pass		

West leads the king of spades and South can see that the contract will depend on making five diamond tricks. On general principles it is good play to duck the first spade. The object is not so much that of a normal hold-up play as to assist declarer to form a picture of the distribution.

South wins the second spade, noting that East showed out. At this point South might say to himself: 'I will play the king of diamonds and then finesse towards East, so that I shall not lose an avalanche of spades.' Or he might say: 'As West has seven spades and East only one, East is likely to have the long diamonds; so I will play East for Q-x-x in diamonds.'

The second line of thought is more intelligent than the first, and many decisions have to be taken on that sort of basis. On this occasion, however, South is in the happy position of being able to test the distribution by playing off his top cards in hearts and clubs. He plays off the ace-king-queen of both suits and discovers that West has a doubleton in each. As West is know to have seven spades – now we see the advantage of the hold-up at the first trick – he can be counted for a doubleton in diamonds.

The next hand is of a commoner type. Declarer cannot obtain a complete count but he can discover a clue that is a better guide than none.

Love All; Dealer North

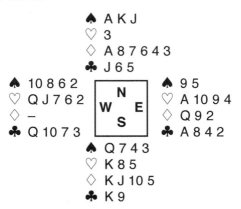

                ♠ A K J
                ♡ 3
                ◇ A 8 7 6 4 3
                ♣ J 6 5
    ♠ 10 8 6 2   ♠ 9 5
    ♡ Q J 7 6 2   ♡ A 10 9 4
    ◇ –   ◇ Q 9 2
    ♣ Q 10 7 3   ♣ A 8 4 2
                ♠ Q 7 4 3
                ♡ K 8 5
                ◇ K J 10 5
                ♣ K 9

North opens One Diamond and East passes. A scientific player would respond One Spade on South's hand, but with so poor a suit the better tactical bid is Two No-Trumps. North should raise to Three, for remember that Three Diamonds would be a sign-off. North should be ready to take a chance on game at no-trumps.

West leads the six of hearts and East wins with the ace. While it is usually correct to return fourth best, East should lead the ten of hearts to the second trick because of its promotional value and because there is a danger that the suit may otherwise become blocked for the defence.

Since he would not fancy a switch to clubs, South may as well win the second heart. The next step should be to play off three rounds of spades. This reveals that East began with a doubleton spade.

Now, which player, if either, is likely to have started with a void in diamonds? If East, then he would have eleven cards in hearts and clubs, including the ace of hearts. With that holding he might have had something to say over the opening One Diamond.

South concludes, therefore, that West is more likely to be short of diamonds than East. So the ace of diamonds is led from dummy and South is careful to drop the jack or ten from hand. When West shows out in diamonds it is simple to take the marked finesse, cash the queen of spades and king of diamonds, and play the five of diamonds to dummy for a total of eleven tricks.

Following a slender clue

As was remarked earlier in this chapter, a complete guess without any clue at all is actually very rare. A well-known American writer made a somewhat rash statement in connection with the following hands:

East/West Game; Dealer West

♠ 3 2
♡ A K 6 4
◇ A K
♣ A 8 7 6 5

♠ K J 10
♡ 3 2
◇ Q J 10 9 7 6
♣ 3 2

The bidding went like this:

West	East
1♣	1◇
2♡	2♠
2NT	3NT
Pass	

East's bid of Two Spades won the writer's commendation, but for my part a straightforward Two No-Trumps would have been just as good. West's rebid of Two Hearts rather than One Heart is open to question, for ace-king alone of partner's suit is not an ideal holding.

North led the queen of hearts and West won. It would have been a mistake to hold off because the opponents might well have switched to spades, attacking the only entry in dummy.

After cashing the top diamonds West led a spade, on which North plays low. West had to decide whether to go up with the king or finesse the jack. The writer's comment on this problem was: 'Which, then, is the correct play? ... Don't ask me. Go and consult a voodoo doctor!'

It is true that West has a guess, but not a complete guess. North has led into a suit bid by declarer. With fewer than five hearts it is more likely that he would have led through dummy's spades. Now with an ace as well as a fair heart suit North might have overcalled the opening One Club with One Heart. As he has not done so, there is a slight indication that South holds the ace of spades and that the jack should be finessed.

This is another hand where the indication, such as it is, would escape any but a perceptive player:

Game All; Dealer West

♠ K 6 3
♡ A 8 2
◇ K 9 7 3
♣ A K 4

♠ A 9 7
♡ J 7 4
◇ A J 10 6
♣ 10 3 2

West opens One No-Trump and East raises to Three No-Trumps. North leads the nine of clubs and a count of tricks reveals that to make game West has to find the queen of diamonds.

The only clue lies in the lead, which appears to be 'top of nothing'. This is confirmed when South plays the eight of clubs on the first round and the five on the second, marking him with Q-J-8-x or Q-J-8-x-x. Now, if North, who appears to have led from 9-x or 9-x-x in clubs, had had a similar holding in diamonds he might have led equally well from that suit. There is therefore a slight negative inference that North holds the critical queen of diamonds. An inference of that sort can very often be drawn when a defender leads from a short suit.

When there is a choice of suits

In the examples so far, declarer has had a choice of finesses in a particular suit. Equally common are hands on which there is a finesse in two or more suits and declarer has to select the right one. The declarer's thinking on the following hand was superficial:

Game All; Dealer South

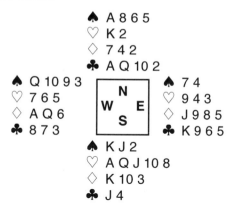

```
              ♠ A 8 6 5
              ♡ K 2
              ◇ 7 4 2
              ♣ A Q 10 2
♠ Q 10 9 3                    ♠ 7 4
♡ 7 6 5          N           ♡ 9 4 3
◇ A Q 6       W     E        ◇ J 9 8 5
♣ 8 7 3          S           ♣ K 9 6 5
              ♠ K J 2
              ♡ A Q J 10 8
              ◇ K 10 3
              ♣ J 4
```

The bidding went:

South	North
1♡	1♠
2♠	3♣
3♡	4♡
Pass	

West led the seven of hearts, which gave nothing away, and South had to decide which black suit to develop. In practice, he took an early finesse of the jack of spades, reflecting that if this lost he would not be exposed to a lead through the king of diamonds. When the spade finesse lost, and later both the king of clubs and ace of diamonds turned up on the wrong side, South was one down, losing a spade, a club, and two diamonds.

Declarer could have made a certainty of this contract by simply drawing trumps and finessing in clubs. The diamond through the king was not a serious threat because by simply covering East's card South could protect himself against the immediate loss of more than two diamond tricks. Once the king of clubs had been forced out, there would be enough tricks for game.

A moderately experienced player, unless very much asleep, would not have made this particular mistake, for he would have known without thinking about it that the diamonds were proof against the loss of three quick tricks. The next hand, though the point is simple enough, would catch many players at the table:

Love All; Dealer South

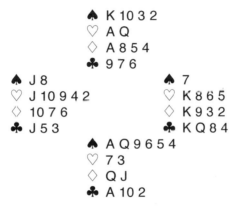

South is in Four Spades and West leads the jack of hearts. At first sight the contract may seem to depend on one of two finesses. If South takes that view, finessing the queen of hearts at trick one, he will go down, for East will surely switch to clubs. There are actually ten sure tricks. South must go up with the ace of hearts, draw trumps, and finesse the queen of diamonds. East makes his two red kings and leads a club. South wins with the ace, cashes the jack of diamonds, and crosses to dummy for the discard of a club on the ace of diamonds.

When to avoid a finesse

The heart finesse on the last hand was wrong because the tricks could be made without risk in another suit. On the following hand the finesse is dangerous because of the possibility of a ruff.

Game All; Dealer South

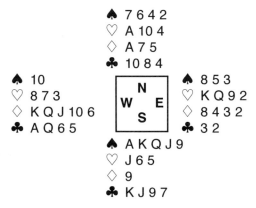

```
              ♠ 7 6 4 2
              ♡ A 10 4
              ◇ A 7 5
              ♣ 10 8 4
  ♠ 10                        ♠ 8 5 3
  ♡ 8 7 3          N          ♡ K Q 9 2
  ◇ K Q J 10 6   W   E        ◇ 8 4 3 2
  ♣ A Q 6 5        S          ♣ 3 2
              ♠ A K Q J 9
              ♡ J 6 5
              ◇ 9
              ♣ K J 9 7
```

South opens One Spade and North raises to Two Spades. South has enough to try for game, either with Three Clubs or Three Spades, and North, having a sound raise, goes to Four Spades.

West lead the king of diamonds and dummy wins. Noting that he has only one other entry to dummy, declarer may take this opportunity to run the ten of clubs, for if East has the queen twice guarded one lead through him will not be enough. In the event, East begins a peter with the three of clubs and West, noticing that the two is missing, continues with the ace of clubs and a third club, which East will ruff. One of dummy's heart losers will go away on the fourth club but there will still be a heart loser and South will be one down.

So long as the trumps are not 4-0 the contract can be made with completely safety. South should draw trumps and lead clubs from hand. He can afford to lose two clubs, for the opponents cannot possibly win two heart tricks before a long club has been established. Say that West wins the first or second round of clubs and leads a heart; East wins with the queen but cannot profitably return a heart. When he comes in with the next club West leads a second heart, but now South goes up with the ace of hearts, crosses to hand with a diamond ruff, and discards the heart loser on the fourth round of clubs.

Had South's clubs on this hand been Q-J-9-7 instead of K-J-9-7 it would not have occurred to him to play in clubs before drawing trumps. In the same sort of way, on this final deal, the queen of diamonds is the temptress that leads South to destruction.

Love All; Dealer South

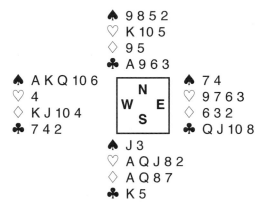

    ♠ 9 8 5 2
    ♡ K 10 5
    ◇ 9 5
    ♣ A 9 6 3

    ♠ A K Q 10 6   ♠ 7 4
    ♡ 4   N   ♡ 9 7 6 3
    ◇ K J 10 4   W   E   ◇ 6 3 2
    ♣ 7 4 2   S   ♣ Q J 10 8

                ♠ J 3
                ♡ A Q J 8 2
                ◇ A Q 8 7
                ♣ K 5

South played in Four Hearts after West had overcalled in spades. The defence began with three top spades, enabling East to discard a diamond.

Realising that he might have to ruff two diamonds, South did not use a trump to enter dummy. Instead, he crossed to the ace of clubs and finessed the queen of diamonds. West won and played a fourth spade, on which East threw his last diamond. Declarer had lost three tricks already and when he played off the ace of diamonds East ruffed.

South was misled by the opportunity to finesse in diamonds. All he had to do, after ruffing the spade at trick three, was play off the ace of diamonds and give up a diamond. Say that West wins and plays a trump; South cashes the top clubs and then continues on cross-ruff lines, trumping the diamond losers with the king and ten of hearts.

If South's diamonds had been A-x-x-x he would surely have followed this line of play. One can add a rider to the verdict of the old lady quoted at the beginning of this chapter. Not only do the experts generally guess right when they have to finesse: they know when it is wrong to finesse at all.

16

Matter of Entry

On many hands declarer can count sufficient tricks for his contract but his difficulty lies in being at the right place sat the right time. In a word, he has entry trouble. On this first hand there is a path to nine tricks but some care must be taken not to block the roadway.

Game All; Dealer South

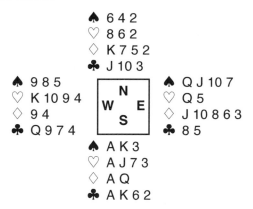

```
              ♠ 6 4 2
              ♡ 8 6 2
              ◇ K 7 5 2
              ♣ J 10 3
  ♠ 9 8 5                    ♠ Q J 10 7
  ♡ K 10 9 4      N          ♡ Q 5
  ◇ 9 4        W     E       ◇ J 10 8 6 3
  ♣ Q 9 7 4       S          ♣ 8 5
              ♠ A K 3
              ♡ A J 7 3
              ◇ A Q
              ♣ A K 6 2
```

South has an obvious Two Club opening and North responds Two Diamonds. A rebid of Two No-Trump by South generally shows about 23–24 points, but although he has a point more than that he is not strong distributionally and Two No-Trump, which partner can pass on a very bad hand, is enough. As it is, North's king and jack-ten entitle him to raise.

On this bidding West might well lead the nine of spades against Three No-Trump, with the general idea of giving nothing away. Counting his top tricks, South can see two in spades, one in hearts, three in diamonds, and three in clubs after the queen has been forced out. That is enough for game, but South must be a little careful how he organises the minor suits. It would be a bad mistake, for example, to play off the ace-king of clubs in the hope of dropping the queen. Instead, South must cash the ace-queen of diamonds and then give up a trick to the queen of clubs, ensuring an entry to dummy so that he can cash the third trick in diamonds.

Of anyone who went down on this hand against a spade lead one would have to say that bridge was not his game, but make the opening lead a low club and it becomes quite easy to go wrong. To put in the jack or ten – a 'free' finesse – is the tiniest bit tempting; but clearly wrong, for it takes the only sure entry off the table before the diamonds can be run. Instead, South must win the first trick with the king of clubs and then follow the same sequence of play as before, using the jack-ten of clubs as an entry.

A similar sort of problem arises on the following hand, though here the defence may allow declarer to escape the consequences of a misplay on the first trick.

Game All; Dealer South

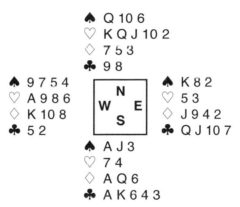

```
              ♠ Q 10 6
              ♡ K Q J 10 2
              ◇ 7 5 3
              ♣ 9 8
  ♠ 9 7 5 4              ♠ K 8 2
  ♡ A 9 8 6      N       ♡ 5 3
  ◇ K 10 8   W     E     ◇ J 9 4 2
  ♣ 5 2          S       ♣ Q J 10 7
              ♠ A J 3
              ♡ 7 4
              ◇ A Q 6
              ♣ A K 6 4 3
```

The best contract, actually, is Four Hearts, but North/South are more likely to finish in Three No-Trump after the following auction:

South	North
1♣	1♡
2NT	3NT
Pass	

West's natural lead after this bidding is the four of spades. With the example of the previous hand before him, the reader will appreciate that South's proper course is to play low from dummy and win with the ace. Then the ace of hearts is forced out and dummy's queen-ten of spades represent a certain entry.

If South makes the mistake of putting on the ten or queen of spades at trick one, East may return the gift by contributing his king. East should note that dummy is short of entries and should retain the king so that he can top dummy's other honour. West will hold up his ace of hearts for one round and dummy will be dead.

Overtaking a high card

An entry problem often arises when there is an unsupported honour opposite a long suit. This can sometimes be solved by overtaking the high card. These are typical combinations:

(i)   A J 10 8 5 3   (ii)   K 10 9 8 4

             K   Q

In diagram (i) suppose that there is only one entry to the long suit. If declarer cannot afford to lose a trick he must cash the king, cross to dummy, and hope to drop the queen under the ace. That is not a particularly good chance and if declarer can afford to give up a trick to the queen his best play will be to overtake the king with the ace and then play the jack. This will establish five tricks whenever the suit is 3-3 or when one defender has Q-x-x-x and the other 9-x.

The combination in diagram (ii) does not look promising, but if dummy has two entries there is a good chance to establish three tricks. The queen must be overtaken by the king and in due course the ace and jack are forced out. If the suit divides 4-3 declarer will lose two tricks and win three.

A more tricky example of this type of play appears in the following hand:

Love All; Dealer South

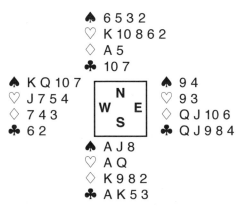

```
                    ♠ 6 5 3 2
                    ♡ K 10 8 6 2
                    ◇ A 5
                    ♣ 10 7
    ♠ K Q 10 7               ♠ 9 4
    ♡ J 7 5 4       N        ♡ 9 3
    ◇ 7 4 3      W     E     ◇ Q J 10 6
    ♣ 6 2           S        ♣ Q J 9 8 4
                    ♠ A J 8
                    ♡ A Q
                    ◇ K 9 8 2
                    ♣ A K 5 3
```

South has enough points for an opening Two No-Trump, but One Club is a better call. North responds One Heart and then South bids Three No-Trump.

West leads the king of spades, East plays the four and South the eight. The hold-up in this situation has the added advantage that it leaves declarer with a major tenace, the ace-jack against the queen-ten, so that West cannot continue the suit without giving up an extra trick. This simple stratagem, known since the earliest days of whist, is dignified by the title, 'Bath Coup'.

From his partner's play of the four West judges that South has the ace-jack, so he switches to a diamond. South plays low from dummy and heads the ten with the king.

Outside the heart suit declarer has five top tricks and little chance of making any more than that. His problem is therefore clearcut: how to make four tricks from hearts.

The obvious play is to lay down the ace-queen of hearts, then cross to the ace of diamonds and lead the king of hearts. That play will succeed if the hearts are 3-3 or if the jack is doubleton. Leading the ace of hearts and overtaking the queen provides an extra chance – that of finding a doubleton nine. South gives up a trick to the jack and makes the last two hearts when he enters dummy with the ace of diamonds.

Entries in the trump suit

When a side suit has to be established in a trump contract declarer may have to postpone drawing trumps in order to conserve essential entries.

North/South Game; Dealer South

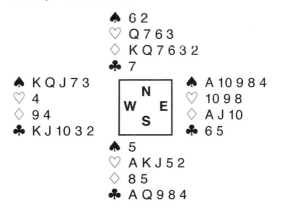

```
              ♠ 6 2
              ♡ Q 7 6 3
              ◇ K Q 7 6 3 2
              ♣ 7
♠ K Q J 7 3        ┌─────┐        ♠ A 10 9 8 4
♡ 4                │  N  │        ♡ 10 9 8
◇ 9 4              │W   E│        ◇ A J 10
♣ K J 10 3 2       │  S  │        ♣ 6 5
                   └─────┘
              ♠ 5
              ♡ A K J 5 2
              ◇ 8 5
              ♣ A Q 9 8 4
```

The bidding goes:

South	West	North	East
1♡	1♠	2♡	3♠
4♡	4♠	5♡	Double
All Pass			

Although uncertain who can make what, North follows the correct policy in a competitive situation of bidding on when in doubt. East cannot be blamed for doubling with his two aces. Perhaps West, at the score, should have taken out the double into Five Spades.

Against Five Hearts doubled West leads the king of spades and follows with a second spade, which South ruffs. South may think first of a cross-ruff. If he makes one club and one diamond trick he will still need to make all his trumps separately. That is unlikely for two reasons: when the opponents come in with the ace of diamonds they can play a trump, and in any case the cards will have to lie very well for South to escape an overruff. As they lie in fact, East will soon overruff in clubs and return a trump.

A much better plan is to establish the diamonds, but this calls for some care regarding entries. First, observe the effect of drawing three rounds of trumps. Then a diamond is led towards the king-queen and West takes the opportunity to begin a peter with the nine, showing a doubleton. East holds off and then the dummy, with only one trump for entry, is dead.

The hand plays quite easily if two heart entries are kept in dummy. A natural sequence would be: ruff the second spade, play one high trump, then a diamond to the king, which is allowed to hold; back to the king of hearts and another diamond; East wins, but as dummy has two entries the diamonds can be established and run.

East/West might have tried a rather different line of defence. Seeing the menace of the diamond suit in dummy, East might have overtaken the spade lead and returned a club with a view to forcing dummy and so reducing the entries. Having the ace of clubs and good trumps South can easily withstand that defence, but on the next hand the policy of forcing dummy to ruff has a better chance of success.

Love All; Dealer South

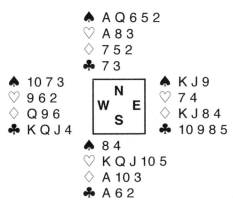

The bidding goes:

South	North
1♡	1♠
2♡	3♡
4♡	Pass

West leads the king of clubs and South wins. There would be no point in holding off and allowing the defence to switch to diamonds.

Counting a club ruff, South can see nine tricks – ten if the spade finesse is right. However, if the spade finesse is wrong South will want to establish a long spade, so the play at trick two should be an immediate spade finesse.

This will lose and the defence may now switch to diamonds. In that case South should win, cash the king-queen of hearts, then lead a spade to the ace and ruff a spade. When the suit breaks he can enter dummy with the ace of hearts to make two long spades.

Better play for the defenders when they take their spade trick is to play on clubs with the idea of forcing dummy to ruff. Suppose that South ruffs the third club on table: then he will have no entry to the long spades in dummy and will be held to nine tricks.

Thus the proper counter to this defence is to refuse the force and throw a diamond from the table – discarding a loser on a loser, as it is called. South can win the next trick and establish the spades as before.

Unblocking for entry

Additional entries can often be obtained by unblocking in a long suit. These are simple examples:

(i)　　　　　A J 8 4　　　　　　(ii)　　　　　　A K 7 5 3
　　10 7 5 2　　　　　9　　　　　　8 2　　　　　　　Q 9
　　　　　　K Q 6 3　　　　　　　　　　　　J 10 6 4

Assume that South, playing no-trumps, requires as many entries as possible to the table. In (i) he leads the king and notes the fall of East's nine. He should follow with the queen and overtake with the ace; then he has a finesse position and can enter dummy twice more via the jack-eight. Note that the same three entries cannot be won, after the fall of the nine, by leading the three to the jack; that will leave South with queen-six and West with ten-seven, and by playing the ten on the subsequent lead of the six, West will kill one of the entries.

In (ii) South begins by leading the ten to the king. Since, after that, one trick must be lost in any event if the suit is not breaking, declarer can play the jack on the next round, overtaking with the ace. As the cards lie, that enables him to enter dummy four times.

On the following hand this sort of manipulation takes place within the trump suit:

Love All; Dealer South

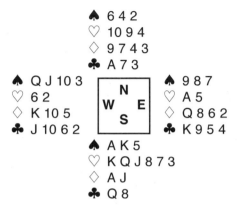

North:
♠ 6 4 2
♡ 10 9 4
◇ 9 7 4 3
♣ A 7 3

West:
♠ Q J 10 3
♡ 6 2
◇ K 10 5
♣ J 10 6 2

East:
♠ 9 8 7
♡ A 5
◇ Q 8 6 2
♣ K 9 5 4

South:
♠ A K 5
♡ K Q J 8 7 3
◇ A J
♣ Q 8

South opens with a bid of Two Hearts, forcing for one round. If he had a doubleton in addition to his ace and useful trump support North would raise to Three Hearts. On his 4-3-3-3 distribution a negative Two No-Trump is better. South rebids Three Hearts and North raises to Four.

West leads the queen of spades and South notes that he has nine tricks on top and is in danger of losing a trick in each suit. The only prospect of a tenth trick lies in finding the king of clubs under the queen. To make anything of that, South will need two entries to dummy, one to lead up to the queen of clubs, one to regain entry and cash the ace.

South might imagine that his best chance to gain entries in the trump suit would be to lead the king in the hope of driving out the ace. That might succeed against moderate defenders but a good player in East's position would take note of the nakedness of dummy apart from the ace of clubs and would hold up his ace.

More accurate play for South, therefore, after winning with the ace of spades, is to lead the seven of hearts and overtake with the nine. East may as well take this and play a second spade. South wins and leads the eight of hearts to dummy's ten. When both opponents follow, the contract depends on finding the club king with East. On the lead of a low club from table East goes up with the king and plays a diamond. South wins, cashes the queen of clubs, and enters dummy with the four of hearts for the discard of one of his losers on the ace of clubs.

Second hand high

There are entry-killing as well as entry-making plays. These often take the form of a high card by second player. Study these common positions:

(iii)　　　 A J 10 6 4　　　　(iv)　　　　　A J 9 6 5

　K 5　　　　　　 Q 7 3　　　 Q 10 3　　　　　　 K 8 4

　　　　 9 8 2　　　　　　　　　　　　7 2

South plays in no-trumps with no side entry to the table. In diagram (iii) he leads the nine, intending to run it; if allowed to do so he will have no difficulty in making four tricks. Correct defence is for West to go up with the king on the first lead; then South must either duck and later lose to the queen, or put on the ace and be cut off from the table when East plays low on the next round.

Diagram (iv) shows a similar position. South leads the two, intending to finesse the nine. If West plays low and East puts on the king, South can make four tricks by finessing on the next round; East can save two of these by allowing the nine to win, but best defence is for West to play the queen on the first round. Then South can make the ace and no more.

Since the mechanics of the game are the same for both sides, declarer can make use of the same kind of play in a situation such as the following:

North/South Game; Dealer North

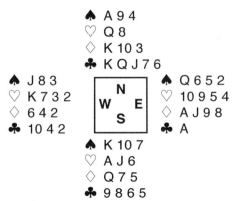

```
                    ♠ A 9 4
                    ♡ Q 8
                    ◇ K 10 3
                    ♣ K Q J 7 6
      ♠ J 8 3          ┌─────┐      ♠ Q 6 5 2
      ♡ K 7 3 2        │  N  │      ♡ 10 9 5 4
      ◇ 6 4 2          │W   E│      ◇ A J 9 8
      ♣ 10 4 2         │  S  │      ♣ A
                       └─────┘
                    ♠ K 10 7
                    ♡ A J 6
                    ◇ Q 7 5
                    ♣ 9 8 6 5
```

The bidding goes:

South	West	North	East
–	–	1♣	Double
Redouble	Pass	Pass	1◇
1NT	Pass	2NT	Pass
3NT	All Pass		

When West leads the six of diamonds South must play 'second hand high', going up with the king. Otherwise East will put in the eight and the defence in due course will make three diamonds, a club and a heart.

After the play of the king of diamonds East will probably win with the ace and switch to a heart. South must not finesse, for that would allow West to play another diamond while the club ace was still out. So South wins the ace of hearts and forces out the ace of clubs. That gives him eight tricks on top and a ninth can be won in hearts.

Blocking play

Another effective way of preventing the run of an adverse suit is by playing a high card that will leave the opponents with a blocked position. Observe these two diagrams:

<pre>
(v)   9 4   (vi)   A 3
      Q 8 3   A 10 7 5 2   K J 8 4 2   Q 5
           K J 6   10 9 7 6
</pre>

In (v) South plays in no-trumps and the suit in question has been bid by East. From three to an honour of partner's suit West leads the three. East plays the ace and returns the five. Now South should read the position and go up with the king; that will prevent the fast run of the suit when the opponents next have the lead.

In (vi) West leads the four against no-trumps. since West would not have led low from a combination headed by king-queen-jack, South knows that one of the top honours is held by East. In that case the play of the ace from dummy on the first lead will surely obstruct the defence. It is obvious that if South plays low from dummy East will win and return the suit, establishing three ready tricks for his partner.

A play based on the same principle appears in the following hand:

Love All; Dealer North

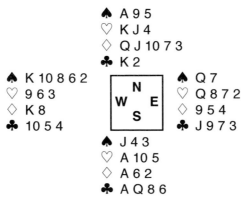

♠ A 9 5
♡ K J 4
◇ Q J 10 7 3
♣ K 2

♠ K 10 8 6 2
♡ 9 6 3
◇ K 8
♣ 10 5 4

♠ Q 7
♡ Q 8 7 2
◇ 9 5 4
♣ J 9 7 3

♠ J 4 3
♡ A 10 5
◇ A 6 2
♣ A Q 8 6

South is in Three No-Trumps and West leads the six of spades. This lead could possibly be from K-Q-8-6 or K-Q-7-6, in which case it would obviously pay to let the six run up to the jack. There are more chances, however, that West has led from only one of the top honours and that East has K-x or Q-x. In that case declarer's best move will be to go up with the ace with a view to blocking the run of the suit.

The play of the ace is especially indicated here because the diamond finesse has to be taken into West's hand. If the important finesse had to be taken in the other direction then East would be able to counter the play of the ace by unblocking with the queen. In the present circumstances that would not avail him.

17
The Danger Hand

One of declarer's commonest problems is to keep a dangerous opponent out of the lead at a particular moment. Many simple and many brilliant plays are directed towards that end. In this first example declarer might not realise that any danger existed.

East/West Game; Dealer North

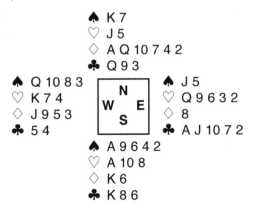

```
              ♠ K 7
              ♡ J 5
              ◇ A Q 10 7 4 2
              ♣ Q 9 3
♠ Q 10 8 3            ♠ J 5
♡ K 7 4        N      ♡ Q 9 6 3 2
◇ J 9 5 3   W     E   ◇ 8
♣ 5 4          S     ♣ A J 10 7 2
              ♠ A 9 6 4 2
              ♡ A 10 8
              ◇ K 6
              ♣ K 8 6
```

The bidding goes:

South	West	North	East
–	–	1◇	Pass
1♠	Pass	2◇	Pass
3NT	All Pass		

Since both his long suits have been called against him West has to choose between a heart and a club. On the whole there is a better chance to find partner with a fair suit in clubs, partly because West has a heart honour himself and partly because East has not had a chance to mention clubs at the one level. Accordingly, West leads the five of clubs, hoping to strike his partner's suit.

South plays low from dummy, and while the orthodox card for East to play is the ten this is an occasion on which a false card of the jack might be tried in order to lull South into false security.

Whichever card is played, South wins with the king and plays king and another diamond. This is the critical point. Although the odds are against a 4-1 break in diamonds, South needs only five tricks from the suit and cannot possibly lose the contract if he finesses the ten. If he does not realise the danger in clubs and plays the top diamond from dummy, sooner or later West will gain the lead and play a club through North's vulnerable queen-nine.

Attacking the danger hand

On many no-trump hands declarer has to force out two defensive winners before he can run his tricks. It may be essential to force out those winners in the right order. Usually the first assault has to be made on what is eventually going to be the danger hand.

Love All; Dealer South

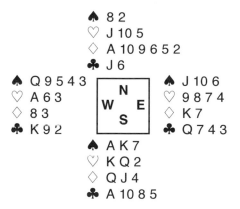

South plays in Three No-Trumps and West leads the four of spades. South holds off the first spade and wins the second. Now observe what will happen if he makes the normal play of establishing his long suit first: a diamond finesse will lose to East, who will clear the spades; declarer will still need a trick from hearts and when West comes in with the ace of hearts he will make two more spades to defeat the contract.

After the play to the first two tricks has placed West with the long spades, South should play first on the suit where West may have the entry. It is clear that West can be kept out of the lead in diamonds, but not in hearts if he holds the ace. At trick three South must lead a heart. West will probably hold off, to conserve his entry. Then South can turn to diamonds with his ninth trick assured.

Conserving partner's entry

On the last hand there was nothing the defence could do if the declarer's timing was right, but often the junior defender, as it were, can protect his partner's entry. There is a lesson for both sides in the following hand:

Love All; Dealer South

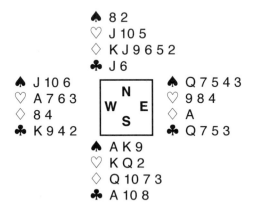

```
              ♠ 8 2
              ♡ J 10 5
              ◇ K J 9 6 5 2
              ♣ J 6
  ♠ J 10 6            ♠ Q 7 5 4 3
  ♡ A 7 6 3    N      ♡ 9 8 4
  ◇ 8 4      W   E    ◇ A
  ♣ K 9 4 2    S      ♣ Q 7 5 3
              ♠ A K 9
              ♡ K Q 2
              ◇ Q 10 7 3
              ♣ A 10 8
```

Again South plays in Three No-Trumps. In many respects the hand resembles the last one, but here it will be observed that East is the player with the long spades and South has to force out two aces, not knowing who has which.

West begins with a short-suit lead of the jack of spades. East plays an encouraging seven and South holds off. West continues with the ten of spades and South wins.

Now from South's point of view the contract will be in danger if one opponent holds five spades and both red aces; also if the aces are divided and he plays on the wrong suit first.

From the play to the first two tricks South should be able to judge that East is the player more likely to hold five spades. (With a suit of J-10-x-x-x West would lead low, and if East had Q-x-x he would play his queen on the second round.) Assuming that the aces are divided, South should want to attack the suit in which East holds his entry.

How the aces lie is a complete guess, but South can give himself an extra chance by leading a low heart at trick three. Suppose that he has guessed wrong (as he has) he may nevertheless be allowed to slip through this heart trick. And that is what will happen unless West is alive and goes up with his ace to clear the spades.

The play of the heart is actually suspicious and would not catch a good player in West's position. When a declarer at no-trumps does not begin to develop a suit like North's diamonds there is generally a tactical reason.

The same sort of play has to be made by a defender on the next hand:

Love All; Dealer South

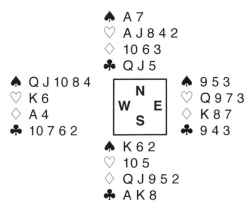

```
              ♠ A 7
              ♡ A J 8 4 2
              ◇ 10 6 3
              ♣ Q J 5
♠ Q J 10 8 4              ♠ 9 5 3
♡ K 6          N          ♡ Q 9 7 3
◇ A 4       W     E       ◇ K 8 7
♣ 10 7 6 2     S          ♣ 9 4 3
              ♠ K 6 2
              ♡ 10 5
              ◇ Q J 9 5 2
              ♣ A K 8
```

The bidding goes:

South	West	North	East
1◇	1♠	2♡	Pass
2NT	Pass	3NT	All Pass

West leads the queen of spades and South wins the second trick on the table. He plays a low diamond from dummy and now the contract can be defeated only if East goes up with the king of diamonds to protect his partner's entry until the spades have been established. This play is not without danger: it would be much easier if East held, for example, A-x in diamonds. Nevertheless, it represents the best chance for the defence.

Exchanging one trick for another

Declarer can sometimes keep a dangerous defender out of the lead by giving up a trick in one suit in exchange for a trick in another.

Game All; Dealer West

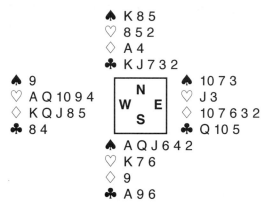

```
                    ♠ K 8 5
                    ♡ 8 5 2
                    ◇ A 4
                    ♣ K J 7 3 2
     ♠ 9                           ♠ 10 7 3
     ♡ A Q 10 9 4      N           ♡ J 3
     ◇ K Q J 8 5    W     E        ◇ 10 7 6 3 2
     ♣ 8 4             S           ♣ Q 10 5
                    ♠ A Q J 6 4 2
                    ♡ K 7 6
                    ◇ 9
                    ♣ A 9 6
```

West opens One Heart, North passes and so does East. South is too strong for a simple bid of One Spade in the protective position. He should bid Two Spades, which North will raise to Four.

West leads the king of diamonds and it is not difficult to see that South is threatened with the loss of a club and three heart tricks. He would like to be able to establish club winners without letting East in to play a heart through the king. This is neatly accomplished by playing a low diamond from dummy on the first trick. Say that West plays another diamond. South discards a club, plays two high trumps from hand, then ace and king of clubs and a club ruff; he returns to dummy with the king of spades and discards two hearts on the established clubs, making an overtrick.

Placing the lead in a single suit

Many manoeuvres to place the lead are possible within the scope of a single suit. For example:

(i)   A Q 6 4   (ii)   Q 10 7 4 3
       K 9 3   J 8 2   K 6   J 9 5
              10 7 5   A 8 2

Suppose that in diagram (i) South wants to establish the thirteenth card but cannot afford to allow East into the lead. Against best defence he can accomplish this only by leading twice towards the ace-queen. If at any point West plays his king he is allowed to hold the trick. If South simply finesses the queen and lays down the ace, West will unblock by throwing his king.

Similarly, in diagram (ii), South wants to set up four tricks without letting East into the lead. To play the ace first is a mistake, for West will throw his king. The only way is to lead low from hand. If West plays the king there is no problem. If West plays the six declarer must go up with the queen and return the three, ducking the next lead into West's hand.

Another factor in these tricky situations is that the defender must not be given a chance to throw his obstructive high card while another suit is being played. That possibility arises on the following hand:

Game All; Dealer South

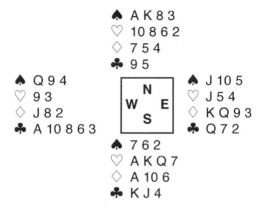

```
              ♠ A K 8 3
              ♡ 10 8 6 2
              ◇ 7 5 4
              ♣ 9 5
♠ Q 9 4                        ♠ J 10 5
♡ 9 3          N               ♡ J 5 4
◇ J 8 2      W   E             ◇ K Q 9 3
♣ A 10 8 6 3    S              ♣ Q 7 2
              ♠ 7 6 2
              ♡ A K Q 7
              ◇ A 10 6
              ♣ K J 4
```

If North/South are going to try for game, Three No-Trumps is a slightly better prospect than Four Hearts.

West leads the six of clubs and East plays the queen. It is sometimes right for declarer to duck with this holding of K-J-x, but that would not be the natural play here. South wins with the king, therefore, and notes that a 3-2 break in hearts will give him eight tricks. The most likely chance of a ninth lies in developing a long spade, but meanwhile East has to be kept out of the lead, for there is an obvious danger that West has several clubs headed by the ace-ten, sitting over South's jack doubleton.

Against moderate opposition South might succeed by playing the ace and king of spades and conceding the third round to West's queen. Good defenders would readily defeat this plan. On the first high spade East would drop the jack as a message to partner that he had the ten as well. Even without this indication West should unblock by dropping the queen on the first or second round of spades.

The situation is similar to that shown in diagram (i) above. At trick two South must lead a low spade to the ace. He returns to hand with a heart and leads another low spade. Unless West puts up the queen (when declarer will duck) the king is played from dummy and the third spade is won, inevitably, by West. Dummy's ten of hearts will be an entry for the thirteenth spade.

A further point to note is that it would be a technical error for South to play off three rounds of hearts after, say, the first round of spades. That would give West a chance to disembarrass himself of the queen of spades on the third heart.

18
Forming a Plan

In a no-trump contract declarer's first concern is usually whether or not to hold up in the suit led; his second, which suit to develop first. Often, as we have seen in the last three chapters, his choice will be determined by considerations of entry or by the need to attack the danger hand. More simply, there may be two possible suits to establish and no special tactical reason for preferring one to the other. Then it will be a question as to which suit is more likely to develop the extra trick. This will often be the suit that is weaker in top cards, as on the following hand:

Game All; Dealer South

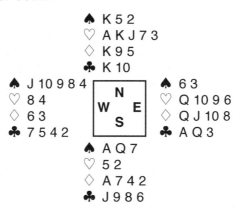

```
                    ♠ K 5 2
                    ♡ A K J 7 3
                    ◇ K 9 5
                    ♣ K 10
      ♠ J 10 9 8 4           ♠ 6 3
      ♡ 8 4          N       ♡ Q 10 9 6
      ◇ 6 3       W   E      ◇ Q J 10 8
      ♣ 7 5 4 2      S       ♣ A Q 3
                    ♠ A Q 7
                    ♡ 5 2
                    ◇ A 7 4 2
                    ♣ J 9 8 6
```

North opens One Heart third in hand. South's best response, especially as he has passed and should not want to risk being left in a contract like Two Clubs, is Two No-Trump. North raises to Three No-Trump and West leads the jack of spades.

South has seven top tricks and can see (if he thinks about it) that two more can surely be established in clubs; not so surely in hearts, for if the queen be wrong and the suit divide 4-2 only one long trick will be forthcoming. Thus, although the hearts appear more glamorous, South should play on clubs, where the tricks he needs can certainly be developed. He may as well go up with the king of spades and lead the king of clubs from the table.

If South tries the other line of play – winning in hand with the queen of spades and finessing the jack of hearts – East, having the hearts and clubs both held, will abandon his partner's spades and play on the solid diamonds.

The right suit to develop on the next hand cannot be so clearly settled.

Love All; Dealer South

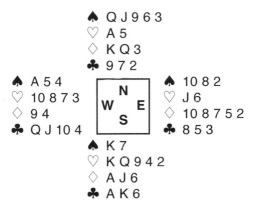

```
                    ♠ Q J 9 6 3
                    ♡ A 5
                    ◇ K Q 3
                    ♣ 9 7 2
   ♠ A 5 4                        ♠ 10 8 2
   ♡ 10 8 7 3        N            ♡ J 6
   ◇ 9 4          W     E         ◇ 10 8 7 5 2
   ♣ Q J 10 4        S            ♣ 8 5 3
                    ♠ K 7
                    ♡ K Q 9 4 2
                    ◇ A J 6
                    ♣ A K 6
```

The orthodox opening on South's hand is One Heart, but Two No-Trump is a fair alternative. North responds Three Spades – forcing for the present. Having nothing in reserve, South bids Three No-Trump. Now it is a fair gamble for North to raise to Six No-Trump. He has 12 points and a good five-card suit; added to South's 20–22, that should produce a play for twelve tricks.

West leads the queen of clubs. Clearly this is not the moment to hold up, so South wins with the ace. Having five top winners in the minor suits he wants to make either five heart and two spade tricks or four spades and three top hearts. In other words, South can make the slam if either suit breaks 3-3 – provided he chooses the right one. Since two tricks will in any event be needed from spades it is natural to play on that suit first. In fact, as a general principle, the suit to play first is usually the one in which top cards are missing; the preceding hand was an example of that.

At trick two, then, South leads the king of spades. If the opponents can be induced to play the ace of spades on the first or second round, or if the ten drops, declarer's task will be simplified. A good player in West's position will not take the ace, however; nor will he play it on the second round when South leads low to the queen.

You see the point of that defence? The spades may be 3-3 but it is dangerous for South to play a third round, for if a defender has held up from A-10-x-x the contract will be down immediately.

South plays a round of hearts next, just in case the jack-ten should be falling in two rounds. When that chance fails he has to decide whether to continue hearts or play a third spade. In favour of playing on hearts is that should the hearts be 4-2 the player with the long heart may not have the ace of spades, in which case it will still be possible to benefit from a 3-3 break in spades. In favour of playing a third spade at once is that an average opponent is more likely to have held off from A-x-x than from A-10-x-x. There is no certain answer; the main lesson of the hand lies in the defensive play of not taking the ace of spades on the first or second round.

Combining the chances in two suits

On the following hand the attempt to combine chances in two suits is more successful:

Game All; Dealer South

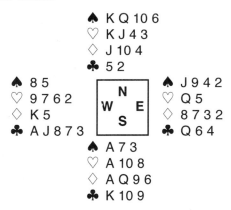

```
                ♠ K Q 10 6
                ♡ K J 4 3
                ◇ J 10 4
                ♣ 5 2
    ♠ 8 5                          ♠ J 9 4 2
    ♡ 9 7 6 2        N             ♡ Q 5
    ◇ K 5        W       E         ◇ 8 7 3 2
    ♣ A J 8 7 3      S             ♣ Q 6 4
                ♠ A 7 3
                ♡ A 10 8
                ◇ A Q 9 6
                ♣ K 10 9
```

South plays in Three No-Trump and West leads the seven of clubs. East plays the queen and South has to win with the king.

It is clear that the diamond finesse, if successful, will produce enough tricks, but South has to consider other possibilities. For example, while to make a fourth spade will not greatly help, four heart tricks will be enough for game.

Before opening up any other suit, declarer must consider whether losing a diamond finesse will necessarily put him down. If the clubs are 4-4 the contract will still be safe, but what are the chances of that? West has led the seven of clubs, remember. If that is fourth best his holding is headed by ace-jack. Players do not usually like to lead from A-J-x-x into a strong hand, so on all grounds it is highly probable that the clubs will be 5-3 or even 6-2.

A heart finesse is in itself no better chance than a diamond finesse, but what South can do is give himself the extra chance of dropping the queen of hearts in two rounds. If that plays fails he can turn to the diamonds. As it happens, the queen of hearts drops doubleton, so without further risk South can make three spades, four hearts, a diamond and a club.

Establishing a trick in a side suit

In trump contracts the problem is not so much which suit to attack first as whether or not to play trumps. This is a simple hand on which playing trumps should be deferred:

Love All; Dealer South

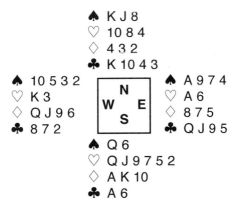

South bids One Heart, North One No-Trump and South Three Hearts. This is a strong invitation to game and as he was up to strength for his direct response North should raise to Four Hearts.

West leads the queen of diamonds and South wins with the ace. South has three top losers and if he plays on trumps at once he may lose a diamond as well as two hearts and a spade. He must set up a spade trick quickly for a diamond discard. The queen of spades is led at trick two, East wins and returns a diamond; now South goes up with the king and takes the discard on the third spade before touching trumps.

Trump leads by the defence

The commonest reason for declarer failing to draw trumps is that he has losers to ruff in the short trump hand. The declarer seeks to play that game on the following hand but the defence has an effective counter.

East/West Game; Dealer North

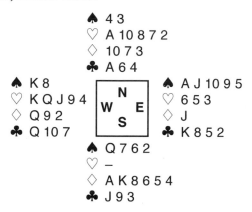

♠ 4 3
♡ A 10 8 7 2
♢ 10 7 3
♣ A 6 4

♠ K 8   ♠ A J 10 9 5
♡ K Q J 9 4   N   ♡ 6 5 3
♢ Q 9 2   W   E   ♢ J
♣ Q 10 7   S   ♣ K 8 5 2

♠ Q 7 6 2
♡ –
♢ A K 8 6 5 4
♣ J 9 3

The bidding goes:

South	West	North	East
–	–	Pass	Pass
1♢	1♡	Double	Pass
2♢	Pass	Pass	2♡
Pass	Pass	3♢	All Pass

After his partner has removed the double of One Heart North does not make the mistake of doubling Two Hearts, which could scarcely be defeated.

West leads the king of hearts against Three Diamonds and on dummy's ace South discards a club rather than a spade, for he has hopes of ruffing spades on the table. To the second trick he leads the four of spades; East plays the nine and is allowed to hold the trick.

Now at bridge what is sauce for the goose is apt to be cyanide for the gander. In other words East can assume that if it does not suit declarer to draw trumps it probably will suit the defence. So at trick three East leads the jack of diamonds. South wins with the ace and plays another spade, taken by West's king. The position is now:

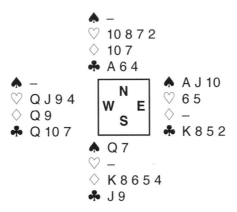

A trump lead by West will apparently give up a trick. In a sense it does, but if West leads the *queen* of diamonds the trick will return twofold. If South wins with the king and draws the last trump he will lose two spades; if he wins and ruffs a spade with the ten of diamonds he will lose a spade and also to the nine of diamonds. A little study will show that in the diagram position the lead of the queen of diamonds by West is the only defence.

Dummy as the master hand

Some hands would be easier to play if one occupied dummy's chair instead of the declarer's. Especially when dummy has the longer trumps it is advisable to study the play 'upside-down', as it were. Played by South, the following hand is deceptive in Six Spades.

Game All; Dealer South

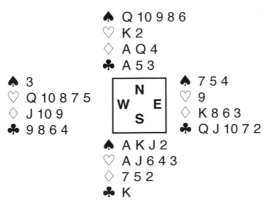

Since his hand is weak for a reverse – that is, for opening One Heart and following with Two Spades – South may prefer to open One Spade. North will force with Three Clubs or Three Diamonds. When South shows a second suit of hearts North will not let the bidding stop short of Six Spades.

West leads the jack of diamonds. South appears to have good chances: he can take the diamond finesse and if that loses he should be able to establish hearts by ruffing two rounds if necessary. The third diamond will go away on the ace of clubs.

This play fails because the hearts are 5-1. Unlucky, but if South mentally stands on his head, viewing the play from North's position, he will see that the contract is a practical certainty.

There is no need even to take the risk that the opening lead may be a singleton. Win with the ace of diamonds, lead a club to the king, return to the eight of spades, and play the ace of clubs, throwing a diamond; then give up a diamond. Say that the opponents play a trump; South overtakes the jack of spades with the queen, ruffs a diamond with the ace of spades, and returns to the king of hearts. A club is ruffed high, the last trump is drawn and dummy is high. Viewed from the North side, it is a simple hand: all declarer has to do is ruff two losers in the short trump hand. At the same time he has to be careful how he manages the spades.

A ruffing finesse

There are more ways to catch a king than by a simple finesse. A final hand shows a new manoeuvre, the ruffing finesse.

North/South Game; Dealer West

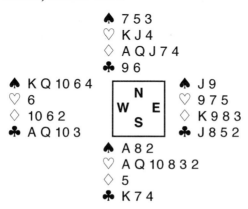

```
                ♠ 7 5 3
                ♡ K J 4
                ◇ A Q J 7 4
                ♣ 9 6
  ♠ K Q 10 6 4           ♠ J 9
  ♡ 6          N         ♡ 9 7 5
  ◇ 10 6 2   W   E       ◇ K 9 8 3
  ♣ A Q 10 3   S         ♣ J 8 5 2
                ♠ A 8 2
                ♡ A Q 10 8 3 2
                ◇ 5
                ♣ K 7 4
```

The bidding goes:

South	West	North	East
–	1♠	Pass	1NT
2♡	Pass	4♡	All Pass

At the score West opens light and East makes a minimum response. When South enters the bidding vulnerable after both opponents have called, North places him with good values and goes straight to game.

West leads the king of spades and East plays the jack. It would be good play for South to duck, for he wants to restrict communication between the defending hands; in particular, he wants to prevent a lead by East through the king of clubs. It is not likely, on the bidding, that West will have six spades.

South wins the second spade and has to consider how to play the diamonds. He can take a direct finesse through West, but a better plan is to go up with the ace and return the queen – a ruffing finesse. If the king appears, South will ruff; if not, he will discard a spade.

East will realise from the play that South has a singleton diamond and probably will not play his king; it may be, from East's point of view, that South will change his mind and ruff.

In practice, South discards a spade and the diamond queen holds. Now declarer ruffs a low diamond, plays ace and another heart, and ruffs a fourth diamond. Then dummy is entered with a third trump and the fifth diamond provides a club discard. South loses just a spade and two clubs.

The play is different in detail if East covers the queen of diamonds, but the result is the same. Note, also, that South would equally have made the contract had the king of diamonds been held by West.

19

The Four Types of End Game

Like chess, bridge has an opening, middle and end game. An endgame situation arises when a defender (or it can be the declarer) is forced to make a disadvantageous lead or play. There are four main types of endplay, conventionally classified as follows:

Throw in, where a defender is forced to lead into a tenace.

Elimination, where a defender has the choice, in a trump contract, of leading into a tenace or making a play that allows declarer to ruff in one hand while he discards a loser from the other.

Trump coup, where a defender's trump tricks are curtailed or made to disappear altogether.

Squeeze, where owing to pressure of space a defender is forced to discard a potential winner.

These descriptions may sound a little abstruse and it is a fact that large books could be (and in some cases have been) written about each one of the four types of ending. Nevertheless, the plays are quite easy to understand in principle.

Throw-in

A defender is endplayed when he is thrown on lead with no alternative but to play into an opponent's tenace combination. This play can take place within a single suit, as in the following example:

7 4 2

K 10 8 6   J 5 3

A Q 9

Declarer leads from dummy and if East plays low puts on the nine from hand. West wins and if no other cards are left has to lead back into the ace-queen. In this example it would not help East to play the jack, for then South would put on the queen and again West would be endplayed.

More often, the lead is thrown in a different suit from that which the defender has to return. In the following example South exits in the suit that the defender has led against no-trumps.

Love All; Dealer South

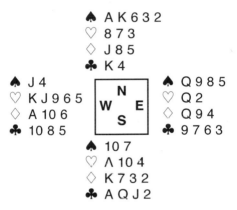

The bidding goes:

South	West	North	East
1♣	1♡	1♠	Pass
1NT	Pass	2NT	All Pass

South has 14 points, but lacking a five-card suit and with only one stop in hearts he should not accept the invitation to game.

West leads the six of hearts, East plays the queen, and South holds off. When East returns the two there is no point in holding up any longer, for no doubt the suit is divided 5-2. The advantage of taking the ace at this point will appear as the play progresses.

South has seven tricks on top but how to make an eighth is not too obvious. No doubt West has the ace of diamonds in addition to three more heart winners, so declarer cannot think of ducking a spade.

South begins by taking four club tricks, West discarding a diamond. That leaves the cards as follows:

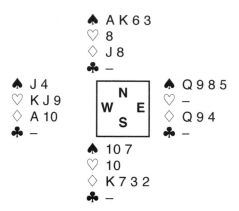

The best chance is to endplay West. First, South must remove possible cards of exit by cashing the ace-king of spades. Then he throws West in with a heart. West makes his three heart tricks and then has to lead from the ace-ten of diamonds into South's king-seven.

Had West's distribution been different – had he had three spades and one diamond left – this play would not have succeeded. As is often the case, declarer has to estimate the probable lie of the adverse cards. If he places West with a singleton ace of diamonds he can make the contract more simply by playing a low diamond.

Elimination

This form of endplay is easier to execute than a throw-in and more reliable in the sense that declarer can often be on a 'sure thing'. In the following end position diamonds are trumps and South can afford to lose two more tricks.

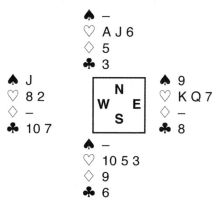

South exits with a club. However the cards lie he can lose only one further trick. Say that West takes the club and leads a heart, which appears to be the best defence. This is won by East's queen and East is then 'on play': he must either lead a heart up to the ace-jack or play a spade which allows South to ruff in one hand while he discards a loser from the other.

The characteristic features of elimination play are the presence of a trump in each hand, none being left in the defending hands; a combination such as the heart holding above where an extra trick must be forthcoming if the opponents have to open it up; a card of exit, such as the club; and the double void in the fourth suit, so that a lead of that suit will permit a ruff and discard.

The term 'elimination' refers not to the extraction of cards from the defending hands but to declarer's elimination of superfluous cards from his own hand and dummy. Note the play of the clubs in the following example:

Game All; Dealer South

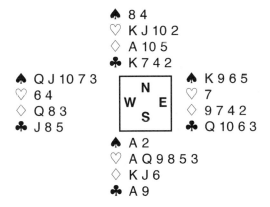

South plays in Six Hearts and West leads the queen of spades. The contract appears to depend on the diamond finesse but in fact it can hardly fail. South wins the ace of spades, draws two top trumps, then plays ace, king and a third club, which he ruffs. He crosses to dummy with a trump and ruffs the fourth club. That leaves:

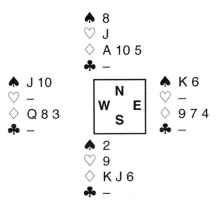

Now it is apparent that South can exit with a spade and lay down his cards in the assurance that he will not be submitted to the hazard of a diamond finesse.

Trump coup

There are many forms of endplay surrounding the trump suit. This is the simplest form of trump coup:

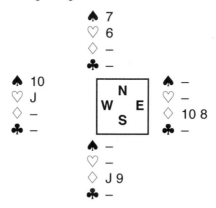

Diamonds are trumps and whether declarer will make one or both of the last two tricks depends on whether the lead is in his own hand or in dummy. If dummy has the lead South can execute a trump coup by leading a plain suit; East has to ruff and South overruffs.

Suppose that a third card were added to this diagram – a winning spade to North and a third trump to South, so that the position was:

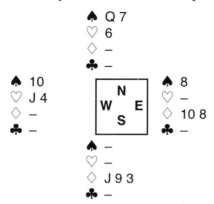

Now it will be observed the South must lose a trick. His third trump is an embarrassment, forcing him to ruff the queen of spades. Thus in preparation for a trump coup it is often necessary for declarer to reduce his trumps to the same number as those held by the right-hand opponent.

Love All; Dealer North

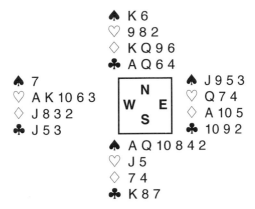

```
              ♠ K 6
              ♡ 9 8 2
              ◇ K Q 9 6
              ♣ A Q 6 4
♠ 7              N           ♠ J 9 5 3
♡ A K 10 6 3   W   E         ♡ Q 7 4
◇ J 8 3 2          S         ◇ A 10 5
♣ J 5 3                      ♣ 10 9 2
              ♠ A Q 10 8 4 2
              ♡ J 5
              ◇ 7 4
              ♣ K 8 7
```

The bidding goes:

South	West	North	East
–	–	1◇	Pass
1♠	Pass	2♣	Pass
3♠	Pass	4♠	All Pass

The defence will probably begin with three rounds of hearts. South ruffs the third round, plays a spade to the king and a spade back to the ace, on which West shows out. Now South plays a diamond to the queen; East wins and returns the ten of diamonds to dummy's king. The position is then:

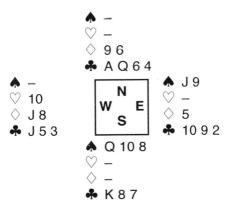

```
              ♠ –
              ♡ –
              ◇ 9 6
              ♣ A Q 6 4
♠ –              N           ♠ J 9
♡ 10           W   E         ♡ –
◇ J 8              S         ◇ 5
♣ J 5 3                      ♣ 10 9 2
              ♠ Q 10 8
              ♡ –
              ◇ –
              ♣ K 8 7
```

The lead is in dummy and at this point declarer must lead a diamond and ruff in order to reduce his trumps to the same number as East's. He follows with three rounds of clubs, finishing in dummy; there is a danger that East will ruff, but that chance has to be taken. When East follows to the clubs the lead is in dummy at trick twelve and declarer makes the last two tricks by way of a trump coup.

Squeeze play

The possibility of squeeze play arises from the simple fact that two hands, those of declarer and dummy, can contain between them more cards than one opponent can hold. The minimum compass is three cards:

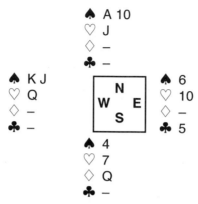

Playing no-trumps, South leads the queen of diamonds. West, having to discard in front of dummy, is squeezed: whichever suit he abandons, North will discard the other. East's cards, in this example, are immaterial.

In the diagram West is threatened by the ace-ten of spades and the jack of hearts. These are described respectively as two-card and one-card menaces. South's four of spades is an entry to the two-card menace. His queen of diamonds is the squeeze card. Those elements are present in every squeeze: two menaces, one of them a two-card menace, lying against one opponent; an entry to the two-card menace; a squeeze card in the hand opposite the two-card menace.

The example above showed a 'one-way' squeeze, in the sense that the squeeze would operate only against West. When the one-card menace is in the same hand as the squeeze card, the squeeze becomes automatic and will work against either opponent. Thus on the following hand it is East who is squeezed:

Game All; Dealer South

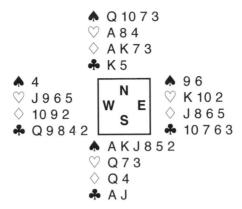

North/South bid as follows:

South	North
1♠	3◇
3♠	4NT
5♡	5NT
7♠	

Once North had bid Five No-Trump, confirming possession of all the aces, South, with all his extra values including the useful queen of diamonds, was prepared to contract for the grand slam.

West led the ten of diamonds and when the dummy goes down South sees that the grand slam is not going to be laydown. The hands do not fit well, both players having a doubleton club.

There are twelve tricks on top and two menace cards – the fourth diamond in dummy and the queen of hearts. If these two menaces are controlled by the same opponent there will be a squeeze.

Declarer wins with the queen of diamonds, draws trumps, and cashes the ace of hearts (an essential move). Then he reduces to the following ending:

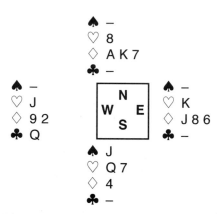

When South plays the last trump, discarding the eight of hearts from the table, East cannot withstand the pressure.

In technical terms this is a 'simple automatic squeeze'. There are also double squeezes in which both opponents are squeezed either simultaneously or on successive tricks; progressive squeezes, ruffing squeezes, suicide squeezes, jettison squeezes and many other varieties.

Appendix 1
The Scoring

Trick score below the line

When a contract has been made the trick score is entered below the line: for each odd trick in the minor suits, clubs and diamonds, 20 points; in the major suits, spades and hearts, 30; for the first trick at no-trumps, 40, for each subsequent trick, 30. Thus, Three No-Trump bid and made scores exactly 100, the amount required for game. A side that has won a game is said to be vulnerable.

When a contract has been doubled these scores below the line are doubled; when redoubled, they are quadrupled.

All other scores are entered above the line.

Bonus for doubled and redoubled contracts

In addition to the points scored in other ways, there is a bonus of 50 for any doubled contract and 100 for any redoubled contract made.

Overtricks

When a contract has not been doubled, overtricks are scored at their simple trick value. Thus, Three Diamonds bid and Five made scores 60 below and 40 above.

When the contract has been doubled, 100 points are scored for each overtrick when not vulnerable, 200 when vulnerable. When the contract has been redoubled, overtricks are 200 not vulnerable, 400 vulnerable.

Penalties for undertricks

When a contract has been defeated, the penalty for each undertrick, undoubled, is 50 when not vulnerable, 100 when vulnerable.

When the contract has been doubled, the penalty for the first undertrick not vulnerable is 100, for the next two undertricks, 200, and for any subsequent undertricks, 300; when vulnerable, for the first trick 200, for each subsequent trick, 300.

When the contract has been redoubled, the amounts set out in the previous paragraph are doubled.

Slam bonuses

The bonus for small slam (twelve tricks) not vulnerable is 500; vulnerable, 750. For a grand slam not vulnerable, 1,000; vulnerable, 1,500.

Game and rubber bonuses

For a rubber won in two games, 700. For a rubber won by two games to one, 500. No bonus points are entered on the score-sheet for the first game by either side.

Honours

When any player (including dummy or a defender) holds four of the five honours in the trump suit, he scores a bonus of 100; when he holds all five honours, 150; when he holds four aces at no-trumps, 150.

Bonuses in an unfinished rubber

When a rubber cannot be completed a side that is a game ahead scores a bonus of 300. A side that has a partscore in an uncompleted game scores 50.

Duplicate Bridge Scoring

In a tournament the various scores are determined at the end of each deal. For example if you bid and make Four Hearts exactly you score +420 non vulnerable, +620 vulnerable. If you make an overtrick the scores will be +450 and +650. Fail by a trick and the penalty will be –50 or –100 depending on the vulnerability. The bonus for bidding and making a slam is calculated in the same way.

Appendix 2
The History of Bridge

Contract bridge is the youngest game of the whist family. Whist is known to have been played in the 17th century. There is no dummy in whist and no bidding; the trump suit is determined by the last card dealt. (The word 'trump' is derived from another game called 'Triumph'.)

Bridge was first heard of at the end of the 19th century. It is thought to have arrived from India and the word itself to come from a Russian game, Biritch, but the dictionaries do not commit themselves on this matter. In the earliest form of bridge the dealer could name the trump suit or pass the option to his partner. The dealer's partner was always dummy. A new feature was the denomination, no-trumps.

The next development was auction bridge, which appeared in about 1910. For the first time there was competitive bidding and a defined contract in place of a simple struggle to make tricks.

In the early 1920s the French game, 'plafond', foreshadowed contract, which itself was first played in America in 1927. The distinguishing feature of contract was that declarer scored below the line only for tricks that he had contracted to make. Other innovations were the factor of vulnerability and big bonuses for slams bid and made.

There have been a few changes in the scoring, though penalties for undertricks and grand slam bonuses have not always been the same.

During the life of contract two more or less new games of the bridge family have been tried out. One was five-suit bridge, introduced in 1938. The fifth suit, royals, ranked between spades and no-trumps. Each player had sixteen cards and the 65th, known as the widow card, could be exchanged by declarer for any card in his hand. The other innovation, rex bridge, was introduced from Sweden in 1958. The pack remained as always but there was a new denomination, rex, in which aces ranked low. Neither of these games created more than then slightest ripple on the pond.

Appendix 3
A Note on the Laws

The laws of bridge are determined by the Portland Club, London, the European Bridge League, the American Contract Bridge League's Laws Commission, and the World Bridge Federations Laws Commission acting in concert. Few players can memorise the whole code. Below is a note on a few of the irregularities that most commonly occur.

Insufficient bid

Any insufficient bid may be accepted by the offenders left hand opponent but otherwise the offender must amend his call in one of the following ways:

(a) By substituting the lowest sufficient non conventional bid in the same denomination – e.g. by amending an insufficient bid of Three Diamonds to Four Diamonds. Penalty: none.

(b) By substituting any other sufficient bid (not a double or redouble, for these are calls, not bids) in the same or another denomination. Penalty: the offender's partner must pass throughout.

(c) By substituting a pass. Penalty: the offender's partner must pass throughout and, in addition, if the offending side becomes the defence, the declarer may call for or prohibit the opening lead of a particular suit.

Penalty card

If a card is exposed by a defender, either accidentally or in committing an irregularity such as a lead out of turn, it may be treated as a penalty card. Penalty cards are designated as either major or minor and must be left face upwards on the table. There are various possibilities surrounding when a penalty card must be played and whether or not the partner of the offender may be required or forbidden to lead the suit of the exposed card.

There is no penalty for the accidental exposure of a card by the declarer.

Lead out of turn

Declarer may accept a defender's lead out of turn; if it was the opening lead, dummy is spread and dummy plays last to the first trick.

Declarer may also elect to spread his hand, becoming dummy while partner becomes declarer.

If declarer does not condone the lead out of turn, the lead reverts to the proper player and the card wrongly led becomes a major penalty card. Alternatively, declarer may allow the offender to pick up his card and may forbid the other defender to lead that suit.

When declarer leads from the wrong hand he may not retract the card unless requested to do so. There is no penalty.

Revoke

A revoke is the failure to follow suit when able to do so. Declarer may ask a defender who has failed to follow suit if he has a card in that suit, and dummy may ask the same question of declarer, but a defender may not ask his partner – although this rule is not enforced in America.

Until established (see below), a revoke may be corrected by the substitution of a correct card. The revoke card, if played by a defender, becomes a penalty card. The non-offending side may withdraw any card it has played after the revoke and before its correction.

A revoke becomes established when the offender or his partner leads or plays to the next trick. (A revoke at the twelfth trick never becomes established; nor is there any penalty for a revoke by dummy.)

The penalty for an established revoke varies. If the offending player won the revoke trick at the end of play that trick is transferred, together with one of any subsequent tricks won by the offending side.

If the offender did not win the trick then if the offending side won that or any other subsequent trick one is transferred at the end of play. However, if the offender wins an additional trick with a card that could have been played to the revoke trick, one such trick is transferred to the other side.

There is no additional penalty for a second revoke in the same suit by the same player.

Claims and concessions

If declarer shows his hand or makes a remark suggesting that he is in a position to claim a number of tricks, play ceases. If the claim is contested the result will be determined by the accuracy of the declarer's initial statement and other factors. My advice is never claim!

A defender who wishes to make a claim or concession can do so by showing his cards to the declarer.

Dummy's rights

Dummy is not permitted to exchange hands with declarer.

Dummy is entitled to draw attention to an irregularity after play has finished or to warn partner against committing an irregularity such as revoking or leading from the wrong hand.

Dummy forfeits these rights if he deliberately looks at any player's cards. If, having forfeited his rights, he warns declarer not to lead from the wrong hand, the opponents may nominate from which hand declarer shall lead. If he assists declarer to correct a revoke, penalty provisions will apply.

Appendix 4
Tournament Bridge

Tournament bridge has been played since before the introduction of contract. It depends on the duplicate principle.

The simplest form of duplicate is a match between two teams of four. Say that four members of the Robinson family are to play a match against four members of the Brown family. Two Robinsons sit North/South at one table, facing two Browns. At the other table the Browns sit North/South, the Robinsons East/West.

A fixed number of hands is played at each table. During the play the cards are not mixed together as in rubber bridge. Each player keeps this own cards in front of him and at the end of the play replaces his thirteen cards in the appropriate slot of a container known as a 'duplicate board'. When, say, eight hands have been played at each table the boards are exchanged. Hands which the Robinsons have held as North/South at one table are held by the Browns at the other. Thus the luck of the deal is in a sense eliminated and a direct comparison of skill can be made.

In duplicate play each hand is a separate entity, with no carry-forward of scores below the line. Dealer and vulnerability are shown on the board. Special bonuses are assigned as follows: 50 for partscore, 300 for non-vulnerable game, 500 for vulnerable game. In most forms of scoring, honours are not counted.

By the use of more elaborate movements, tournaments can be conducted for any number of teams or pairs, and even to produce an individual winner.

Tournament bridge is organised at every level from club events up to the world championship. There is a World Bridge Federation, a European Bridge League, and in Britain each country has its own Union.

Appendix 5
Glossary

above the line – all scores other than for tricks bid and made are entered above the horizontal line across the centre of the score-sheet

auction – the period during which the bidding takes place

auction bridge – a game that preceded contract

below the line – scores in respect of tricks bid and made are entered below the line on the score-sheet

bid – an undertaking by a player to win a specified number of tricks either with no trumps or with a specified suit as trumps

business double – old term for penalty double

call – a comprehensive term including any bid, double, redouble or pass

cash – play off a winning card

chicane – an old term meaning a void suit

competitive bidding – an auction in which both sides take part

contract – the final bid of the auction, which may be doubled or redoubled, determines the contract in which the hand has to be played

convention – an arrangement between partners whereby a bid or play has a particular, possibly artificial, meaning

cue-bid – a bid that shows a controlling card rather than a genuine suit

cut – the division of the pack into two parts when presented to the dealer

deal – the distribution of the cards in rotation to the players; also used as equivalent to 'hand', signifying the lay-out of the four hands and the bidding and play thereof

declarer – the player who, having been first to name the denomination that wins the final contract, plays both his partner's cards (the dummy) and his own

defender – in bidding, the side that did not open the bidding is the defending side; in play, the partners in opposition to the declarer are the defenders

discard – the play of a card that is not of the suit led and not a trump

distribution – the manner in which suits are divided in a single player's hand, or in which a suit is divided round the table

double – a call that has the effect of increasing penalties if a contract is not made or of increasing the premium score if it is made; by convention, a double may be for penalties or for take-out, requesting partner to bid

doubleton – a holding of two cards of a suit

duck – the play of a low card for tactical reasons when a higher card is held

dummy – the partner of the player who becomes declarer; his hand, which is exposed on the table after the opening lead

duplicate – form of competitive bridge in which the same hands are replayed at two or more tables

echo – method of signalling in defence by playing a high card followed by a lower one of the same suit

elimination – process of eliminating suits in preparation for an endplay

endplay – tactical situation towards the end of a hand, particularly situations in which a defender has to make a disadvantageous lead

entry – a winning card that affords entry to a player's hand

exit – to play a card that relinquishes the lead

false card – a card played with deceptive intent, generally a card that departs from convention

finesse – an attempt to win or establish a trick by playing a card that is not the highest held

force – in bidding, a call that conventionally compels partner to respond; in play, the lead of a card that forces an opponent to ruff if he wants to win the trick

free bid – a free bid, raise, rebid or response, is one that follows an intervening bid by the right-hand opponent

free double – a double which, if the contract is made, will not have the effect of doubling opponents into game

game – a side that scores 100 points below the line wins a game *grand slam* – the winning of all thirteen tricks by one side

hold-up – tactical manoeuvre of declining to win a trick

honour – an ace, king, queen, jack or ten

informatory double – old term for take-out double

insufficient bid – an illegal call that is not sufficient to overcall the previous bid

intermediates – useful cards such as eights and nines

jump bid – a bid that is higher – generally one trick higher – than is required to overcall the previous bid

lead – to play the first card to a trick; the card so played

major suit – spades and hearts, whereof a contract at the four level wins game

minor suit – diamonds and clubs, whereof a contract at the five level wins game

negative response – one that by convention denies certain values

odd tricks – tricks won by declarer in excess of six

opener – the player who makes the first bid of the auction

overbid, overcall – in so far as distinction is observed, an overbid is an injudiciously high call, an overcall a bid by the defending side after the bidding has been opened

overtrick – each odd trick beyond those for which declarer has contracted

partscore – a score below the line insufficient for game

pass – call signifying that a player does not wish to bid, double or redouble; often expressed by the words 'no bid'

penalty – points lost by a side that has failed to make a contract

penalty card – a card exposed by a defender other than in the normal course of play and subject to penalty

penalty double – a double whose primary object is to extract penalties

peter – same as echo

plain suit – not the trump suit

point count – method of valuation by assigning points to high cards

positive response – one that by convention proclaims certain values

pre-emptive bid – bid at a high level made with the object of shutting out the opponents

premium score – all points scored other than those below the line

prepared bid – one chosen so that the player will be able to bid accurately on the next round

protective bid – one made in he last position, following two passes, and based on the presumption that partner has undisclosed strength

psychic bid – a bluff bid

raise – direct support for partner, as by raising One Spade to Two Spades

rebid – bid made in the same denomination as the player's previous bid; also, any bid on the second round made by the opener

redouble – call that can be made only following an opponent's double, increasing penalties if the contract fails, and increasing trick score and bonuses if the contract succeeds

re-open – to make a bid or double in the last position at a point when the bidding would otherwise have ended

responder – in the absence of qualification, the partner of the opening bidder

revoke – failure to follow suit when able to do so

rubber – period of play that ends when a side has won two games

ruff – to play a trump when a plain suit has been led

sacrifice – bid that deliberately incurs a penalty

side suit – suit other than the trump suit (same as plain suit)

sign-off – bid proclaiming weakness, usually inviting partner to pass

singleton – a holding of one card in a suit

slam – contract to make twelve tricks, a small slam, or thirteen tricks, a grand slam

squeeze – situation in which a player is forced to discard winners or cards that protect winners

take-out double – double that by convention asks partner to bid

tenace – combination of cards, such as ace-queen, whose trick-winning power depend on the lie of the cards and who has the lead

trick – the lead and the three cards that follow form a trick *trump* – suit with superior rank named in the contract; a card of that suit; to play such a card (equals ruff)

unblock – to play or discard a card that would otherwise prevent the run of a suit or win an unwelcome trick

underbid – a call that understates the value of the hand; also, in Law, an insufficient bid

undertrick – tricks whereby declarer falls short of his contract

void – to be void of a suit is to have no cards in it

vulnerable – state of pair that has won a game, whereafter penalties are increased

Yarborough – hand containing no card higher than a nine